Retirement Income Roadmap

A guide to income, savings, and next steps

Kayla Price

This book is intended for educational and informational purposes only. It is not a substitute for professional legal, tax, financial, insurance, medical, Medicare, Medicaid, Social Security, retirement, or investment advice. Rules, costs, program details, product availability, and annual figures may change. Always verify current information with the appropriate qualified professional before making decisions.

For additional educational resources, visit:

priceservicesgroup.com

Price Services Group, L.L.C.

info@priceservicesgroup.com | 1-866-648-1578

Printed in the United States of America. First Edition, 2026

Important Disclaimer

This guide is for educational purposes only. It is not legal, tax, investment, financial, insurance, retirement, Social Security, or Medicare advice. The information in this book is general in nature and may not apply to your individual circumstances.

Nothing in this guide creates an attorney-client relationship, financial planning relationship, investment advisory relationship, insurance advisory relationship, or any other professional relationship unless separately agreed in writing. Readers should consult qualified legal, tax, financial, insurance, Social Security, Medicare, and retirement professionals before making decisions.

Price Services Group, L.L.C. is not affiliated with or endorsed by Medicare, the Centers for Medicare & Medicaid Services (CMS), Social Security, the Social Security Administration (SSA), or any other government agency.

Insurance and annuity guarantees are based on the financial strength and claims-paying ability of the issuing carrier. Annuities are not deposits, are not FDIC-insured, and may be subject to surrender charges, fees, limitations, exclusions, and tax consequences.

Product availability and suitability vary by state, carrier, product, and individual circumstances. No product or strategy is right for everyone. Examples in this guide are hypothetical and educational only. They are not promises, projections, guarantees, or recommendations.

Before acting on anything discussed in this book, schedule time with qualified professionals who can review your specific goals, income sources, assets, liabilities, health concerns, tax situation, family needs, and risk tolerance.

A Note Before You Begin

Retirement planning can feel bigger than it needs to feel. Many people reach their fifties, sixties, or early retirement years with savings, accounts, statements, and good intentions, but without one clear picture of how their money will actually become dependable income.

This book was written to slow the conversation down. It is meant to help you understand the major moving pieces: Social Security, Medicare, retirement accounts, safe money strategies, annuities, taxes, healthcare costs, spouse protection, long-term care concerns, and legacy goals. It is not meant to make you your own advisor, insurance professional, tax preparer, attorney, or Medicare specialist.

The real value of retirement income planning is not memorizing every technical rule. The value is seeing how decisions connect. A Social Security decision can affect withdrawals. A Medicare premium can affect cash flow. A market loss can feel different when you are withdrawing income than it did when you were still working. A surviving spouse may need a plan that works when only one set of decisions remains.

At Price Services Group, L.L.C., the guiding phrase is simple: Where You Matter. That phrase matters because retirement planning is personal. Numbers matter, but the person behind the numbers matters more. The goal is to help you ask better questions, organize your thoughts, and feel prepared for a thoughtful planning conversation.

As you read, underline what sounds familiar. Circle the questions that make you pause. Make notes in the margin. Then bring those notes to a retirement income review. If you would like help seeing how your income sources fit together, you can schedule a personalized planning conversation at https://host.safemsngr.com/widget/bookings/psglifeandretirementplan.

How to Use This Book

You do not have to read this book in one sitting. In fact, it may be more useful if you do not. Retirement income planning is easier when you take one topic at a time and give yourself room to think.

The first chapters explain why retirement income planning is different from saving for retirement. The middle chapters introduce the risks that can pressure income, including market loss, inflation, longevity, withdrawal risk, healthcare costs, and long-term care needs. The later chapters help you think about protection, legacy, common mistakes, and what to gather before a planning review.

This is an educational book, not a workbook. Still, you may want to keep a separate notebook nearby. When a chapter sounds like your situation, write down the issue in plain language. For example: "I am not sure when we should claim Social Security," or "We need to know what happens to income if one of us passes away first."

Try not to use the book to diagnose yourself too quickly. Two households can have the same account balance and need very different plans. One may have a pension, another may not. One may have large healthcare costs, another may have family support concerns. One may care most about guaranteed income, while another may value flexibility.

The best use of this book is to become a more confident participant in the conversation. You should finish with a clearer understanding of the issues and a stronger sense of what needs to be reviewed before decisions are made.

Table of Contents

Chapter One

Building Your Income Roadmap

Clarifying income sources, savings, and next steps.

Kayla Price

Chapter 1: Retirement Income Without the Overwhelm

This opening chapter matters because many people come to retirement with scattered information but no simple income picture.

Retirement income planning begins by turning confusion into a calm sequence of questions.

The First Step Is Not a Product

Retirement income planning often begins best with a blank page and a careful conversation. Before anyone talks about a product, rate, account, or strategy, the household needs to understand what income is required and what risks could interrupt it.

The first planning win is often a one-page income picture. A household may have five or six accounts, two Social Security estimates, an old life policy, a Medicare folder, and a few strong opinions from friends. None of those pieces are bad, but they can feel noisy until someone organizes them by purpose: dependable income, flexible savings, emergency money, protection, and legacy goals.

In a review, this part of the roadmap is connected back to the household's income needs, tax picture, risk comfort, liquidity, spouse protection, and future flexibility. The goal is to understand how the first step is not a product affects the broader plan before a decision is made.

The important issue is connection. A decision that seems small by itself can affect income, taxes, risk, spouse protection, healthcare flexibility, or future choices.

A better approach is to bring the question into the open. A review can sort what is clear, what needs confirmation, and what should be coordinated with another qualified professional.

The useful planning move is to connect the topic to real household cash flow. If the decision changes monthly income, liquidity, taxes, spouse protection, healthcare flexibility, or legacy intentions, it deserves a place on the roadmap.

From Piles of Paper to One Picture

Most people have pieces of a plan. They have statements, benefit estimates, insurance policies, tax returns, and maybe a rough monthly budget. What they often do not have is one coordinated picture showing how the pieces work together.

A product-first conversation can make people feel as if they are being pushed toward an answer before the question is clear. A better starting place is the household rhythm: what comes in, what must go out, what changes after work ends, and what would create stress if it happened at the wrong time.

In a review, this part of the roadmap is connected back to the household's income needs, tax picture, risk comfort, liquidity, spouse protection, and future flexibility. The goal is to understand how from piles of paper to one picture affects the broader plan before a decision is made.

The important issue is connection. A decision that seems small by itself can affect income, taxes, risk, spouse protection, healthcare flexibility, or future choices.

A better approach is to bring the question into the open. A review can sort what is clear, what needs confirmation, and what should be coordinated with another qualified professional.

The useful planning move is to connect the topic to real household cash flow. If the decision changes monthly income, liquidity, taxes, spouse protection, healthcare flexibility, or legacy intentions, it deserves a place on the roadmap.

Confidence Comes From Order

Confidence is not the same as certainty. No plan can remove every unknown. But a clear roadmap can help you know what is expected, what is protected, what is flexible, and what should be revisited.

Clarity also means naming what is not yet known. No one knows future tax law, market returns, health needs, or family emergencies with certainty. That is why a retirement roadmap should be reviewed, not framed as a one-time prediction.

In a review, this part of the roadmap is connected back to the household's income needs, tax picture, risk comfort, liquidity, spouse protection, and future flexibility. The goal is to understand how confidence comes from order affects the broader plan before a decision is made.

The important issue is connection. A decision that seems small by itself can affect income, taxes, risk, spouse protection, healthcare flexibility, or future choices.

A better approach is to bring the question into the open. A review can sort what is clear, what needs confirmation, and what should be coordinated with another qualified professional.

The useful planning move is to connect the topic to real household cash flow. If the decision changes monthly income, liquidity, taxes, spouse protection, healthcare flexibility, or legacy intentions, it deserves a place on the roadmap.

A Client-Style Example

Dana and Mark have several accounts, one small pension, and Social Security estimates, but they cannot tell whether the money will feel steady month to month.

Dana and Mark do not need a thicker binder. They need a simple retirement income snapshot showing what is guaranteed, what is flexible, what is exposed to the market, and what should be left alone for emergencies.

The lesson is not that every reader with a similar story needs the same answer. The lesson is that personal context changes the planning conversation.

If a scenario feels familiar, it is worth writing down what part caught your attention and bringing that note to a review.

Common Misunderstandings

A common misconception is that organization comes after decisions. In reality, organization often comes first.

Another is that confusion means a person is behind. Often it simply means the pieces have never been put on one page.

A third misunderstanding is assuming the chapter topic can be decided by a rule of thumb. A rule of thumb may start a conversation, but it cannot replace a review of income need, time horizon, health, family priorities, tax status, and comfort with tradeoffs.

What People Often Overlook

People overlook how much relief comes from seeing the plan in plain English.

They may also overlook small obligations, such as insurance premiums or family support, that affect monthly comfort.

People also overlook how this issue interacts with the rest of the plan and how much relief can come from seeing the plan in plain English.

People also overlook how this issue interacts with the rest of the plan. They may also overlook small obligations, such as insurance premiums or family support, that affect monthly comfort.

What a Planning Review Usually Looks At

A clarity review usually starts by collecting the pieces and arranging them by purpose:

current and future income sources, including Social Security, pension income, employment income, annuity income, and portfolio withdrawals

essential expenses, lifestyle expenses, healthcare costs, debt payments, family support, charitable goals, and emergency reserves

account types, tax treatment, beneficiary designations, liquidity needs, market exposure, and protection strategies

insurance coverage, life insurance, long-term care concerns, Medicare planning, survivor income needs, and legacy intentions

The review should connect decisions rather than treating each topic as a separate island.

If your information feels scattered, bring the statements you have and schedule a conversation at https://host.safemsngr.com/widget/bookings/psglifeandretirementplan.

Questions to Bring Into the Conversation

Use these questions as conversation starters for your own situation:

What income do we need every month before optional spending begins?

Which parts of our current plan are clear, and which parts are still scattered?

What would make us feel more organized before we retire or before we make our next decision?

They are not do-it-yourself instructions; they are prompts to bring into a qualified review.

A Calm Planning Note

The first review should reduce the noise. When the pieces are organized by purpose, the household can see what needs attention now and what can wait.

A calm planning conversation should make the next step feel clearer. It may lead to action, or it may simply identify what should be watched, verified, or discussed with a tax, legal, Medicare, Social Security, or insurance professional.

Advisor Perspective: Starting With the Household

A retirement income roadmap should begin with the household, not the account statement. Two families can have the same savings balance and need different plans because their lives are different. One household may have a pension, low debt, and modest spending. Another may have aging parents, adult children who still need help, a mortgage, and health concerns. A balance alone cannot show those differences.

That is why an advisor-led review often begins with ordinary questions. What feels secure? What feels confusing? What bills must be covered every month? What spending could pause if conditions changed? What would the household want protected even if it meant giving up some upside? These questions make the plan personal without turning the conversation into a sales pitch.

If the reader feels overwhelmed, the best next step is not to solve everything at once. The best next step is to gather the major pieces and let a qualified professional help organize them.

Small clarity can change the whole tone of the retirement conversation.

It can also help spouses talk to each other. One person may be focused on safety, while the other may be focused on opportunity. One may worry about healthcare, while the other worries about leaving money to family. A roadmap gives those concerns a shared language, so the conversation becomes less about who is right and more about what the household needs the plan to accomplish.

That shared language is often the first real relief.

It makes the next conversation easier.

And more honest.

Chapter Summary

This chapter's key point is that retirement income without the overwhelm should be reviewed in context, not as an isolated decision.

The reader does not need to leave with a product decision. The better goal is to leave with clearer questions and a stronger understanding of what personal review should cover.

Next, the book looks at why the paycheck years and retirement years require different planning habits.

Chapter 2: Why Retirement Planning Changes When the Paycheck Stops

The paycheck years and the retirement years are not the same financial season.

When earned income stops, the plan must replace a paycheck, absorb surprises, and reduce avoidable pressure on savings.

A Different Kind of Math

During the working years, mistakes can often be softened by the next paycheck. In retirement, the margin for error can feel smaller because savings may need to create income while also staying available for later needs.

A paycheck does more than deposit money. It creates timing. It tells the mortgage, grocery bill, utilities, and weekend plans when cash will arrive. Retirement removes that familiar rhythm, so the plan has to create a new one with Social Security, pensions, interest, annuity income, withdrawals, cash reserves, or some combination of sources.

In a review, this part of the roadmap is connected back to the household's income needs, tax picture, risk comfort, liquidity, spouse protection, and future flexibility. The goal is to understand how a different kind of math affects the broader plan before a decision is made.

The important issue is connection. A decision that seems small by itself can affect income, taxes, risk, spouse protection, healthcare flexibility, or future choices.

A better approach is to bring the question into the open. A review can sort what is clear, what needs confirmation, and what should be coordinated with another qualified professional.

The useful planning move is to connect the topic to real household cash flow. If the decision changes monthly income, liquidity, taxes, spouse protection, healthcare flexibility, or legacy intentions, it deserves a place on the roadmap.

The Emotional Side of Spending

Many good savers are surprised by how difficult it feels to spend from accounts they spent decades building. A plan can make spending feel more intentional and less like guessing.

The change can be emotional. People who were excellent savers may feel uneasy taking withdrawals, even when they planned for retirement for years. That hesitation is not irrational. It is the mind noticing that the old refill system has changed.

In a review, this part of the roadmap is connected back to the household's income needs, tax picture, risk comfort, liquidity, spouse protection, and future flexibility. The goal is to understand how the emotional side of spending affects the broader plan before a decision is made.

The important issue is connection. A decision that seems small by itself can affect income, taxes, risk, spouse protection, healthcare flexibility, or future choices.

A better approach is to bring the question into the open. A review can sort what is clear, what needs confirmation, and what should be coordinated with another qualified professional.

The useful planning move is to connect the topic to real household cash flow. If the decision changes monthly income, liquidity, taxes, spouse protection, healthcare flexibility, or legacy intentions, it deserves a place on the roadmap.

When Income Has to Be Built

Some retirees have pensions, many do not, and some have only partial guaranteed income. The question becomes how to combine reliable income with flexible assets in a way that fits the household.

A strong retirement income plan respects both the math and the feeling. It should show which bills are covered by predictable income, which expenses can flex, and which assets should not be tapped casually.

In a review, this part of the roadmap is connected back to the household's income needs, tax picture, risk comfort, liquidity, spouse protection, and future flexibility. The goal is to understand how when income has to be built affects the broader plan before a decision is made.

The important issue is connection. A decision that seems small by itself can affect income, taxes, risk, spouse protection, healthcare flexibility, or future choices.

A better approach is to bring the question into the open. A review can sort what is clear, what needs confirmation, and what should be coordinated with another qualified professional.

The useful planning move is to connect the topic to real household cash flow. If the decision changes monthly income, liquidity, taxes, spouse protection, healthcare flexibility, or legacy intentions, it deserves a place on the roadmap.

A Client-Style Example

Evelyn retired after decades of steady deposits, then realized that choosing which account to spend from each month felt very different from saving into those accounts.

Evelyn's review starts by mapping the month. Social Security arrives on one date, a pension on another, and withdrawals may be needed quarterly. Seeing the timing reduces the fear that every bill requires a new investment decision.

The lesson is not that every reader with a similar story needs the same answer. The lesson is that personal context changes the planning conversation.

If a scenario feels familiar, it is worth writing down what part caught your attention and bringing that note to a review.

Common Misunderstandings

Many retirees assume spending will feel natural once work stops. Good savers often need time to adjust.

Another mistake is treating every withdrawal as a failure instead of part of a planned paycheck replacement system.

A third misunderstanding is assuming the chapter topic can be decided by a rule of thumb. A rule of thumb may start a conversation, but it cannot replace a review of income need, time horizon, health, family priorities, tax status, and comfort with tradeoffs.

What People Often Overlook

The timing of deposits and withdrawals matters.

Cash reserves can prevent a retiree from treating every bill as an investment decision.

People also overlook how this issue interacts with the rest of the plan. The timing of deposits and withdrawals matters.

People also overlook how this issue interacts with the rest of the plan. Cash reserves can prevent a retiree from treating every bill as an investment decision.

What a Planning Review Usually Looks At

A paycheck-replacement review looks closely at timing and reliability:

current and future income sources, including Social Security, pension income, employment income, annuity income, and portfolio withdrawals

essential expenses, lifestyle expenses, healthcare costs, debt payments, family support, charitable goals, and emergency reserves

account types, tax treatment, beneficiary designations, liquidity needs, market exposure, and protection strategies

insurance coverage, life insurance, long-term care concerns, Medicare planning, survivor income needs, and legacy intentions

The review should connect decisions rather than treating each topic as a separate island.

If you are not sure how your paycheck will be replaced, use https://host.safemsngr.com/widget/bookings/psglifeandretirementplan to request a retirement income conversation.

Questions to Bring Into the Conversation

Use these questions as conversation starters for your own situation:

How will our monthly income arrive once employment income stops?

Which expenses must be covered by dependable income, and which expenses can remain flexible?

How much cash reserve would help us avoid selling assets under pressure?

They are not do-it-yourself instructions; they are prompts to bring into a qualified review.

A Calm Planning Note

Replacing a paycheck is both a cash-flow exercise and a comfort exercise. The plan should show how money arrives without making every month feel improvised.

A calm planning conversation should make the next step feel clearer. It may lead to action, or it may simply identify what should be watched, verified, or discussed with a tax, legal, Medicare, Social Security, or insurance professional.

The Paycheck Replacement Conversation

The paycheck years train people to think in deposits. Retirement asks them to think in systems. A paycheck arrives because work was performed. Retirement income may arrive because of Social

Security rules, pension elections, annuity contracts, interest credits, dividends, withdrawals, cash reserves, or tax decisions. The source changes, and so does the responsibility.

One practical exercise is to separate income into three groups: dependable income, planned withdrawals, and flexible spending. Dependable income might include Social Security, pension income, or contractually guaranteed income backed by an issuing carrier. Planned withdrawals may come from retirement accounts or taxable accounts. Flexible spending includes travel, gifts, projects, and other items that can be adjusted if needed.

This does not make retirement risk-free. It makes the cash-flow picture easier to discuss. When the reader knows which income is steady and which income depends on other factors, the household can make calmer decisions.

Chapter Summary

This chapter's key point is that why retirement planning changes when the paycheck stops should be reviewed in context, not as an isolated decision.

The reader does not need to leave with a product decision. The better goal is to leave with clearer questions and a stronger understanding of what personal review should cover.

Next, the focus shifts from saving money to intentionally creating income.

Chapter 3: The Difference Between Saving Money and Creating Income

A balance on a statement is not the same as an income plan.

Accumulation asks how to grow money; income planning asks how to turn resources into spendable cash flow that can last.

A Balance Is Only a Starting Point

An account balance tells you what exists today. It does not tell you how much can be safely drawn, what taxes may apply, what happens during a market decline, or how income changes for a surviving spouse.

Saving is measured by balances. Income design is measured by reliability, timing, taxes, and sustainability. A seven-figure statement may still leave a retiree wondering what can be spent this month. A smaller balance paired with pension income, Social Security, and disciplined reserves may feel more stable than expected.

In a review, this part of the roadmap is connected back to the household's income needs, tax picture, risk comfort, liquidity, spouse protection, and future flexibility. The goal is to understand how a balance is only a starting point affects the broader plan before a decision is made.

The important issue is connection. A decision that seems small by itself can affect income, taxes, risk, spouse protection, healthcare flexibility, or future choices.

A better approach is to bring the question into the open. A review can sort what is clear, what needs confirmation, and what should be coordinated with another qualified professional.

The useful planning move is to connect the topic to real household cash flow. If the decision changes monthly income, liquidity, taxes, spouse protection, healthcare flexibility, or legacy intentions, it deserves a place on the roadmap.

Income Needs a Sequence

A retirement income strategy usually looks at which dollars are used first, which dollars are protected, which dollars remain invested, and which dollars are reserved for emergencies or future care.

The practical question is not simply, 'How much do I have?' It is, 'Which dollars are meant to do which job?' Dollars used for next year's income may need different treatment than dollars intended for ten years from now, future care, or beneficiaries.

In a review, this part of the roadmap is connected back to the household's income needs, tax picture, risk comfort, liquidity, spouse protection, and future flexibility. The goal is to understand how income needs a sequence affects the broader plan before a decision is made.

The important issue is connection. A decision that seems small by itself can affect income, taxes, risk, spouse protection, healthcare flexibility, or future choices.

A better approach is to bring the question into the open. A review can sort what is clear, what needs confirmation, and what should be coordinated with another qualified professional.

The useful planning move is to connect the topic to real household cash flow. If the decision changes monthly income, liquidity, taxes, spouse protection, healthcare flexibility, or legacy intentions, it deserves a place on the roadmap.

The Plan Should Match the Person

Some people value the highest possible growth. Others value predictability. Many want a mix. The right conversation starts with goals, not assumptions.

Creating income also means deciding what happens when conditions are imperfect. If markets are down, taxes change, a spouse gets sick, or a major repair appears, the income plan should offer options instead of forcing one painful move.

In a review, this part of the roadmap is connected back to the household's income needs, tax picture, risk comfort, liquidity, spouse protection, and future flexibility. The goal is to understand how the plan should match the person affects the broader plan before a decision is made.

The important issue is connection. A decision that seems small by itself can affect income, taxes, risk, spouse protection, healthcare flexibility, or future choices.

A better approach is to bring the question into the open. A review can sort what is clear, what needs confirmation, and what should be coordinated with another qualified professional.

The useful planning move is to connect the topic to real household cash flow. If the decision changes monthly income, liquidity, taxes, spouse protection, healthcare flexibility, or legacy intentions, it deserves a place on the roadmap.

A Client-Style Example

Robert has a large retirement account, but he is uneasy because he does not know what amount he can withdraw without creating problems later.

Robert's balance is encouraging, but his confidence improves only after the money is divided by purpose: near-term withdrawals, emergency cash, longer-term growth, and possible protected income.

The lesson is not that every reader with a similar story needs the same answer. The lesson is that personal context changes the planning conversation.

If a scenario feels familiar, it is worth writing down what part caught your attention and bringing that note to a review.

Common Misunderstandings

A large balance does not automatically create a dependable income stream.

A withdrawal rate is not a full plan unless taxes, timing, risk, and cash reserves are considered.

A third misunderstanding is assuming the chapter topic can be decided by a rule of thumb. A rule of thumb may start a conversation, but it cannot replace a review of income need, time horizon, health, family priorities, tax status, and comfort with tradeoffs.

What People Often Overlook

Tax character matters. Traditional, Roth, taxable, insurance, and annuity dollars may behave differently.

The order of withdrawals can affect both confidence and taxes.

People also overlook how this issue interacts with the rest of the plan. Tax character matters. Traditional, Roth, taxable, insurance, and annuity dollars may behave differently.

People also overlook how this issue interacts with the rest of the plan. The order of withdrawals can affect both confidence and taxes.

What a Planning Review Usually Looks At

An income-design review asks which dollars should do which job:

current and future income sources, including Social Security, pension income, employment income, annuity income, and portfolio withdrawals

essential expenses, lifestyle expenses, healthcare costs, debt payments, family support, charitable goals, and emergency reserves

account types, tax treatment, beneficiary designations, liquidity needs, market exposure, and protection strategies

insurance coverage, life insurance, long-term care concerns, Medicare planning, survivor income needs, and legacy intentions

The review should connect decisions rather than treating each topic as a separate island.

If you have savings but no clear income design, a personal review can help connect the pieces: https://host.safemsngr.com/widget/bookings/psglifeandretirementplan.

Questions to Bring Into the Conversation

Use these questions as conversation starters for your own situation:

Which dollars are intended for near-term income, future income, emergencies, and legacy goals?

Do we understand the tax treatment of each account we may use for income?

What withdrawal pattern would be reasonable to discuss with our tax and financial professionals?

They are not do-it-yourself instructions; they are prompts to bring into a qualified review.

A Calm Planning Note

Income design gives savings a job description. That job description helps the household avoid using long-term money for short-term pressure without realizing it.

A calm planning conversation should make the next step feel clearer. It may lead to action, or it may simply identify what should be watched, verified, or discussed with a tax, legal, Medicare, Social Security, or insurance professional.

Why the Income Design Has to Be Personal

Income design should not be copied from a neighbor, a headline, or a simple online calculator. A calculator may estimate a number, but it cannot fully understand a spouse with health concerns, a desire to help grandchildren, a family history of longevity, a large taxable account, or anxiety about market loss.

The income conversation should also consider the order of spending. Some dollars may be better used early, while others may be better left to grow or remain protected. Some withdrawals may increase taxable income. Some account types may affect future tax planning. Some products may create income but limit access. These details do not need to be frightening, but they should be visible before decisions are made.

Visibility helps families avoid rushed choices.

The goal is a plan the household can actually live with. A mathematically elegant strategy that makes the retiree nervous every month may not be the right strategy. A clear income design should be practical enough to follow.

Chapter Summary

This chapter's key point is that the difference between saving money and creating income should be reviewed in context, not as an isolated decision.

The reader does not need to leave with a product decision. The better goal is to leave with clearer questions and a stronger understanding of what personal review should cover.

Next, Social Security enters the picture as one of the most important income sources many retirees will have.

Chapter 4: Social Security as Part of the Income Picture

Social Security is often one of the most important income sources in retirement, but it should not be viewed by itself.

The timing decision connects to work income, spouse benefits, survivor needs, taxes, withdrawals, and longevity expectations.

Timing Is More Than an Age

The claiming age is important, but it is not the whole decision. A household should also consider health, work plans, spouse benefits, survivor benefits, taxes, and how withdrawals may fill the gap if benefits are delayed.

Social Security timing is often discussed as if there is one correct age. In real households, timing depends on work plans, health, spouse age differences, survivor needs, taxes, and how much savings would be used while waiting. The right conversation compares tradeoffs rather than chasing a universal answer.

In a review, this part of the roadmap is connected back to the household's income needs, tax picture, risk comfort, liquidity, spouse protection, and future flexibility. The goal is to understand how timing is more than an age affects the broader plan before a decision is made.

For Social Security, the important issue is coordination. Claiming decisions may interact with work income, spouse benefits, survivor benefits, tax exposure, and withdrawals from other accounts.

A better approach is to bring the question into the open. A review can sort what is clear, what needs confirmation, and what should be coordinated with another qualified professional.

The useful planning move is to connect the topic to real household cash flow. If the decision changes monthly income, liquidity, taxes, spouse protection, healthcare flexibility, or legacy intentions, it deserves a place on the roadmap.

The Survivor Lens

For married couples, Social Security timing can affect the income available to the surviving spouse. That makes the decision more than an individual choice.

For couples, the survivor issue deserves special attention. When one spouse dies, the household may keep the larger of two Social Security benefits, not both. That means the claiming decision can affect the income available to the person who lives longer.

In a review, this part of the roadmap is connected back to the household's income needs, tax picture, risk comfort, liquidity, spouse protection, and future flexibility. The goal is to understand how the survivor lens affects the broader plan before a decision is made.

For Social Security, the important issue is coordination. Claiming decisions may interact with work income, spouse benefits, survivor benefits, tax exposure, and withdrawals from other accounts.

A better approach is to bring the question into the open. A review can sort what is clear, what needs confirmation, and what should be coordinated with another qualified professional.

The useful planning move is to connect the topic to real household cash flow. If the decision changes monthly income, liquidity, taxes, spouse protection, healthcare flexibility, or legacy intentions, it deserves a place on the roadmap.

Avoiding Isolated Decisions

Social Security should not be claimed simply because a birthday arrives or a friend claimed at the same age. The benefit is part of a larger income picture.

A review should use current benefit estimates and current rules, then flag anything that needs confirmation with Social Security or another qualified professional before a claim is filed.

In a review, this part of the roadmap is connected back to the household's income needs, tax picture, risk comfort, liquidity,

spouse protection, and future flexibility. The goal is to understand how avoiding isolated decisions affects the broader plan before a decision is made.

For Social Security, the important issue is coordination. Claiming decisions may interact with work income, spouse benefits, survivor benefits, tax exposure, and withdrawals from other accounts.

A better approach is to bring the question into the open. A review can sort what is clear, what needs confirmation, and what should be coordinated with another qualified professional.

The useful planning move is to connect the topic to real household cash flow. If the decision changes monthly income, liquidity, taxes, spouse protection, healthcare flexibility, or legacy intentions, it deserves a place on the roadmap.

A Client-Style Example

Linda wants to claim early because she is tired of waiting, while her spouse is concerned about the survivor income that may remain later.

Linda and her spouse compare more than monthly benefit amounts. They look at the income gap, the survivor picture, and how withdrawals might change if one spouse waits.

The lesson is not that every reader with a similar story needs the same answer. The lesson is that personal context changes the planning conversation.

If a scenario feels familiar, it is worth writing down what part caught your attention and bringing that note to a review.

Common Misunderstandings

The highest monthly benefit is not always the only goal.

Claiming because a friend claimed at the same age ignores spouse, survivor, tax, and cash-flow differences.

A third misunderstanding is assuming the chapter topic can be decided by a rule of thumb. A rule of thumb may start a

conversation, but it cannot replace a review of income need, time horizon, health, family priorities, tax status, and comfort with tradeoffs.

People also misunderstand Social Security as an isolated government benefit. In practice, it often becomes the foundation that other income decisions are built around.

What People Often Overlook

Spouse and survivor benefits can be more important than the first monthly check.

Work income and taxes may complicate a decision that looks simple.

People also overlook how this issue interacts with the rest of the plan. Spouse and survivor benefits can be more important than the first monthly check.

People also overlook how this issue interacts with the rest of the plan. Work income and taxes may complicate a decision that looks simple.

What a Planning Review Usually Looks At

A review for this topic usually focuses on the facts that affect the household's next decision:

current and future income sources, including Social Security, pension income, employment income, annuity income, and portfolio withdrawals

essential expenses, lifestyle expenses, healthcare costs, debt payments, family support, charitable goals, and emergency reserves

account types, tax treatment, beneficiary designations, liquidity needs, market exposure, and protection strategies

insurance coverage, life insurance, long-term care concerns, Medicare planning, survivor income needs, and legacy intentions

For Social Security, the review may compare claiming ages and discuss how benefits fit with other income sources, while avoiding promises about future rules or personal tax outcomes.

If Social Security timing is still a question, bring your current estimates to a review scheduled at https://host.safemsngr.com/widget/bookings/psglifeandretirementplan.

Questions to Bring Into the Conversation

Use these questions as conversation starters for your own situation:

How would claiming earlier or later affect the rest of our income plan?

What happens to household income if one spouse dies first?

Should we review benefit estimates before making a permanent claiming decision?

They are not do-it-yourself instructions; they are prompts to bring into a qualified review.

A Calm Planning Note

Social Security decisions can feel urgent because the claiming ages are familiar and the benefit estimate is easy to see. Even so, the best timing conversation is usually broader than the benefit amount on one page. It should consider the income gap before claiming, survivor protection, taxes, work plans, and the role of other assets.

A calm planning conversation should make the next step feel clearer. It may lead to action, or it may simply identify what should be watched, verified, or discussed with a tax, legal, Medicare, Social Security, or insurance professional.

Social Security as a Planning Anchor

For many retirees, Social Security is the closest thing to a foundation in the income plan. It is not usually enough by itself, but it may cover a meaningful portion of essential spending. That makes the timing decision important, especially for households without pensions.

The claiming conversation should be connected to the rest of the roadmap. If a person claims earlier, savings may not have to cover as many bridge years, but the monthly benefit may be lower than if claiming were delayed. If a person waits, the household may need another income source during the waiting period. For couples, the survivor benefit can make the decision even more personal.

Because Social Security rules can be detailed and personal, readers should verify their own estimates and options before filing. The book's job is to show why the decision matters; the review's job is to connect the decision to the household.

That confirmation matters.

Especially before filing.

It deserves care.

And careful review.

Chapter Summary

This chapter's key point is that social security as part of the income picture should be reviewed in context, not as an isolated decision.

The reader does not need to leave with a product decision. The better goal is to leave with clearer questions and a stronger understanding of what personal review should cover.

Next, the conversation turns to Medicare and healthcare costs, because income planning must account for medical cash flow.

Chapter 5: Medicare, Healthcare Costs, and Retirement Cash Flow

Healthcare is not separate from retirement income; it is one of the regular claims on that income.

Medicare decisions can affect premiums, out-of-pocket exposure, prescription costs, provider access, and cash flow confidence.

Premiums Are Only One Piece

Retirees often focus on monthly premiums, but healthcare cash flow can also include deductibles, copays, prescriptions, dental care, vision care, hearing care, travel coverage, and out-of-network exposure.

Healthcare belongs in the cash-flow plan because it arrives as real bills, not as a footnote. Premiums, prescriptions, dental work, hearing aids, vision care, copays, deductibles, and travel-related coverage questions can all affect how much spendable income remains.

In a review, this part of the roadmap is connected back to the household's income needs, tax picture, risk comfort, liquidity, spouse protection, and future flexibility. The goal is to understand how premiums are only one piece affects the broader plan before a decision is made.

For healthcare, the important issue is realism. Premiums and out-of-pocket expenses should be treated as recurring retirement costs, not rare exceptions.

A better approach is to bring the question into the open. A review can sort what is clear, what needs confirmation, and what should be coordinated with another qualified professional.

The useful planning move is to connect the topic to real household cash flow. If the decision changes monthly income, liquidity, taxes, spouse protection, healthcare flexibility, or legacy intentions, it deserves a place on the roadmap.

Medicare Is Important, Not Automatic Planning

Medicare can be valuable, but it does not eliminate healthcare planning. Choices about coverage can affect both access and spending.

Medicare choices also shape daily life. A plan that looks inexpensive may not fit a favorite doctor, medication list, travel pattern, or tolerance for out-of-pocket exposure. The planning issue is not only cost; it is fit.

In a review, this part of the roadmap is connected back to the household's income needs, tax picture, risk comfort, liquidity, spouse protection, and future flexibility. The goal is to understand how medicare is important, not automatic planning affects the broader plan before a decision is made.

For healthcare, the important issue is realism. Premiums and out-of-pocket expenses should be treated as recurring retirement costs, not rare exceptions.

A better approach is to bring the question into the open. A review can sort what is clear, what needs confirmation, and what should be coordinated with another qualified professional.

The useful planning move is to connect the topic to real household cash flow. If the decision changes monthly income, liquidity, taxes, spouse protection, healthcare flexibility, or legacy intentions, it deserves a place on the roadmap.

Healthcare Costs Need a Line on the Map

A realistic income plan gives healthcare its own place. It does not hide medical costs inside a vague emergency category.

Because Medicare rules and premiums can change, this part of the manuscript should always be reviewed before publication and before any reader makes an enrollment decision.

In a review, this part of the roadmap is connected back to the household's income needs, tax picture, risk comfort, liquidity, spouse protection, and future flexibility. The goal is to understand

how healthcare costs need a line on the map affects the broader plan before a decision is made.

For healthcare, the important issue is realism. Premiums and out-of-pocket expenses should be treated as recurring retirement costs, not rare exceptions.

A better approach is to bring the question into the open. A review can sort what is clear, what needs confirmation, and what should be coordinated with another qualified professional.

The useful planning move is to connect the topic to real household cash flow. If the decision changes monthly income, liquidity, taxes, spouse protection, healthcare flexibility, or legacy intentions, it deserves a place on the roadmap.

A Client-Style Example

Sam budgeted for travel and home projects, then discovered that premiums, dental care, and prescriptions needed a more realistic place in the plan.

Sam's plan improves when healthcare is no longer treated as a vague surprise. Prescriptions, premiums, dental work, and possible out-of-pocket costs receive their own place in the spending estimate.

The lesson is not that every reader with a similar story needs the same answer. The lesson is that personal context changes the planning conversation.

If a scenario feels familiar, it is worth writing down what part caught your attention and bringing that note to a review.

Common Misunderstandings

Medicare does not mean healthcare is free.

A low premium may not be the best fit if provider access, prescriptions, or out-of-pocket exposure create stress.

A third misunderstanding is assuming the chapter topic can be decided by a rule of thumb. A rule of thumb may start a

conversation, but it cannot replace a review of income need, time horizon, health, family priorities, tax status, and comfort with tradeoffs.

People sometimes assume Medicare means healthcare is free. Medicare can be important, but premiums, prescriptions, dental care, and other out-of-pocket expenses can still affect the income plan.

What People Often Overlook

Dental, vision, hearing, and prescription costs deserve attention.

IRMAA and other Medicare-related cost issues should be reviewed with current rules.

People also overlook how this issue interacts with the rest of the plan. Dental, vision, hearing, and prescription costs deserve attention.

People also overlook how this issue interacts with the rest of the plan. IRMAA and other Medicare-related cost issues should be reviewed with current rules.

What a Planning Review Usually Looks At

A review for this topic usually focuses on the facts that affect the household's next decision:

current and future income sources, including Social Security, pension income, employment income, annuity income, and portfolio withdrawals

essential expenses, lifestyle expenses, healthcare costs, debt payments, family support, charitable goals, and emergency reserves

account types, tax treatment, beneficiary designations, liquidity needs, market exposure, and protection strategies

insurance coverage, life insurance, long-term care concerns, Medicare planning, survivor income needs, and legacy intentions

For Medicare and healthcare, the review may identify questions about enrollment timing, coverage type, prescriptions, providers, premiums, and out-of-pocket exposure.

If healthcare costs are hard to place in your retirement budget, you can start a planning conversation at https://host.safemsngr.com/widget/bookings/psglifeandretirementplan.

Questions to Bring Into the Conversation

Use these questions as conversation starters for your own situation:

Have we budgeted for premiums, prescriptions, dental, vision, hearing, and out-of-pocket costs?

Do our Medicare choices fit our doctors, medications, travel patterns, and cash flow?

What healthcare costs are predictable, and what costs require a reserve?

They are not do-it-yourself instructions; they are prompts to bring into a qualified review.

A Calm Planning Note

Healthcare planning can feel frustrating because the choices are detailed and the language is unfamiliar. A calm review does not try to make you an expert in every Medicare rule. It helps you understand what questions affect your doctors, prescriptions, premiums, travel, and cash flow.

A calm planning conversation should make the next step feel clearer. It may lead to action, or it may simply identify what should be watched, verified, or discussed with a tax, legal, Medicare, Social Security, or insurance professional.

Healthcare Costs Belong in the Monthly Plan

Healthcare planning often becomes clearer when it is moved from the emergency category into the monthly income conversation.

Premiums, prescriptions, dental care, eye care, hearing needs, and expected copays may not all arrive at once, but they still compete for retirement income.

Medicare decisions can also affect lifestyle. A retiree who travels frequently may care about different features than someone who sees several local specialists. A person with expensive prescriptions may need a careful drug review. Someone with a tight monthly budget may focus on premium predictability and out-of-pocket exposure.

This is an area where current-year review matters. Medicare rules, plan availability, formularies, premiums, provider networks, and IRMAA-related issues should be checked with qualified professionals and current materials before decisions are made.

Chapter Summary

This chapter's key point is that medicare, healthcare costs, and retirement cash flow should be reviewed in context, not as an isolated decision.

The reader does not need to leave with a product decision. The better goal is to leave with clearer questions and a stronger understanding of what personal review should cover.

Next, the book looks at market losses and why retirement withdrawals can change the risk conversation.

Chapter 6: The Risk of Market Losses in Retirement

Market losses feel different when withdrawals are happening at the same time.

Sequence of returns risk means the order of gains and losses can matter as much as the average return.

The Order of Returns Matters

If losses happen early in retirement while withdrawals continue, the account may have fewer dollars left to participate in a later recovery. This is sequence of returns risk in everyday language.

Sequence of returns risk is simple in plain English: bad market years hurt more when they happen while you are taking money out. If withdrawals continue during a decline, the account has fewer dollars left to participate in a later recovery.

In a review, this part of the roadmap is connected back to the household's income needs, tax picture, risk comfort, liquidity, spouse protection, and future flexibility. The goal is to understand how the order of returns matters affects the broader plan before a decision is made.

For market risk, the important issue is timing. A loss in the first years of retirement can be more damaging than the same loss during the saving years because withdrawals may continue while values are down.

A better approach is to bring the question into the open. A review can sort what is clear, what needs confirmation, and what should be coordinated with another qualified professional.

The useful planning move is to connect the topic to real household cash flow. If the decision changes monthly income, liquidity, taxes, spouse protection, healthcare flexibility, or legacy intentions, it deserves a place on the roadmap.

Income Money May Need Different Rules

Money intended for near-term income may need a different risk conversation than money intended for long-term growth or legacy.

This does not mean retirees must avoid investing. It means income money and long-term growth money may need different expectations. A retiree might keep some assets positioned for growth while protecting or reserving dollars needed for near-term spending.

In a review, this part of the roadmap is connected back to the household's income needs, tax picture, risk comfort, liquidity, spouse protection, and future flexibility. The goal is to understand how income money may need different rules affects the broader plan before a decision is made.

For market risk, the important issue is timing. A loss in the first years of retirement can be more damaging than the same loss during the saving years because withdrawals may continue while values are down.

A better approach is to bring the question into the open. A review can sort what is clear, what needs confirmation, and what should be coordinated with another qualified professional.

The useful planning move is to connect the topic to real household cash flow. If the decision changes monthly income, liquidity, taxes, spouse protection, healthcare flexibility, or legacy intentions, it deserves a place on the roadmap.

Risk Tolerance Can Change

A person who felt comfortable with market swings while working may feel differently once those same accounts are paying the bills.

The advisor's role is often to slow down panic. A written income strategy can help a household know which dollars are available for the next few years and which dollars are intended to wait through volatility.

In a review, this part of the roadmap is connected back to the household's income needs, tax picture, risk comfort, liquidity, spouse protection, and future flexibility. The goal is to understand how risk tolerance can change affects the broader plan before a decision is made.

For market risk, the important issue is timing. A loss in the first years of retirement can be more damaging than the same loss during the saving years because withdrawals may continue while values are down.

A better approach is to bring the question into the open. A review can sort what is clear, what needs confirmation, and what should be coordinated with another qualified professional.

The useful planning move is to connect the topic to real household cash flow. If the decision changes monthly income, liquidity, taxes, spouse protection, healthcare flexibility, or legacy intentions, it deserves a place on the roadmap.

A Client-Style Example

A couple retires into a down market and keeps withdrawing the same amount, which can make recovery harder even if the market later improves.

In a down market, the couple's biggest risk is not a scary statement. It is being forced to sell long-term assets for current income. A reserve strategy gives them more choices.

The lesson is not that every reader with a similar story needs the same answer. The lesson is that personal context changes the planning conversation.

If a scenario feels familiar, it is worth writing down what part caught your attention and bringing that note to a review.

Common Misunderstandings

Average return does not tell the whole retirement story.

Risk tolerance during working years may not match risk tolerance when the portfolio is paying bills.

A third misunderstanding is assuming the chapter topic can be decided by a rule of thumb. A rule of thumb may start a conversation, but it cannot replace a review of income need, time horizon, health, family priorities, tax status, and comfort with tradeoffs.

People often think average return tells the whole story. In retirement, the order of returns can matter because withdrawals may lock in losses during difficult years.

What People Often Overlook

A cash buffer may be as important emotionally as it is mathematically.

Rebalancing and withdrawal timing should not be improvised during a downturn.

People also overlook how this issue interacts with the rest of the plan. A cash buffer may be as important emotionally as it is mathematically.

People also overlook how this issue interacts with the rest of the plan. Rebalancing and withdrawal timing should not be improvised during a downturn.

What a Planning Review Usually Looks At

A market-risk review tests how withdrawals may behave during difficult markets:

current and future income sources, including Social Security, pension income, employment income, annuity income, and portfolio withdrawals

essential expenses, lifestyle expenses, healthcare costs, debt payments, family support, charitable goals, and emergency reserves

account types, tax treatment, beneficiary designations, liquidity needs, market exposure, and protection strategies

insurance coverage, life insurance, long-term care concerns, Medicare planning, survivor income needs, and legacy intentions

The review should connect decisions rather than treating each topic as a separate island.

If market losses would affect your retirement paycheck, make that concern part of your review: https://host.safemsngr.com/widget/bookings/psglifeandretirementplan.

Questions to Bring Into the Conversation

Use these questions to talk about volatility before markets are stressful:

Which assets could be affected by a market decline during the first years of retirement?

Do we have a plan for income if markets are down when withdrawals are needed?

How much volatility can we emotionally and financially tolerate?

They are not do-it-yourself instructions; they are prompts to bring into a qualified review.

A Calm Planning Note

Market risk does not mean every retiree should avoid the market. It means the income plan should respect the difference between money that can wait and money that may be needed soon. That distinction can help reduce emotional decisions during difficult markets.

A calm planning conversation should make the next step feel clearer. It may lead to action, or it may simply identify what should be watched, verified, or discussed with a tax, legal, Medicare, Social Security, or insurance professional.

When Losses Meet Withdrawals

Market declines are uncomfortable at any age, but they can be especially damaging when the retiree is also taking income. During the working years, a person may be able to wait, keep contributing, and let time do some of the repair work. In retirement, withdrawals may continue even while the account is down. That combination can change the recovery path.

A plain-language way to explain sequence risk is to imagine drawing water from a reservoir during a drought. If rain returns quickly, the reservoir may recover. If withdrawals continue while the drought lasts, there is less water left when the rain comes back. The same idea can apply to investment accounts during early retirement losses.

This is why some households use cash reserves, protected income, or conservative buckets for near-term spending. The purpose is not to eliminate every market risk. The purpose is to reduce the chance that a retiree must sell growth assets at an especially bad time.

That simple distinction can protect confidence.

Chapter Summary

This chapter's key point is that the risk of market losses in retirement should be reviewed in context, not as an isolated decision.

The reader does not need to leave with a product decision. The better goal is to leave with clearer questions and a stronger understanding of what personal review should cover.

Next, inflation, longevity, and the cost of waiting add another layer to the roadmap.

Chapter 7: Inflation, Longevity, and the Cost of Waiting

Retirement can last longer than expected, and costs rarely stand still.

Inflation risk, longevity risk, and delay can quietly reshape what income must do over decades.

Long Life Is a Blessing and a Planning Challenge

Many people hope for a long retirement, but a long retirement requires income that can keep working through changing costs and changing needs.

Inflation and longevity are quiet risks because they rarely announce themselves all at once. A grocery bill rises, an insurance premium changes, a home repair costs more than expected, and suddenly an income amount that once felt comfortable feels tighter.

In a review, this part of the roadmap is connected back to the household's income needs, tax picture, risk comfort, liquidity, spouse protection, and future flexibility. The goal is to understand how long life is a blessing and a planning challenge affects the broader plan before a decision is made.

The important issue is connection. A decision that seems small by itself can affect income, taxes, risk, spouse protection, healthcare flexibility, or future choices.

A better approach is to bring the question into the open. A review can sort what is clear, what needs confirmation, and what should be coordinated with another qualified professional.

The useful planning move is to connect the topic to real household cash flow. If the decision changes monthly income, liquidity, taxes, spouse protection, healthcare flexibility, or legacy intentions, it deserves a place on the roadmap.

Inflation Is Quiet Until It Is Not

Inflation does not usually arrive as one dramatic bill. It shows up in groceries, insurance, utilities, repairs, taxes, and services.

Longevity risk is not a fear of living long. It is the planning challenge of making sure money, coverage, and decision-making support can last for a long life. A longer retirement gives both investments and expenses more time to surprise the household.

In a review, this part of the roadmap is connected back to the household's income needs, tax picture, risk comfort, liquidity, spouse protection, and future flexibility. The goal is to understand how inflation is quiet until it is not affects the broader plan before a decision is made.

The important issue is connection. A decision that seems small by itself can affect income, taxes, risk, spouse protection, healthcare flexibility, or future choices.

A better approach is to bring the question into the open. A review can sort what is clear, what needs confirmation, and what should be coordinated with another qualified professional.

The useful planning move is to connect the topic to real household cash flow. If the decision changes monthly income, liquidity, taxes, spouse protection, healthcare flexibility, or legacy intentions, it deserves a place on the roadmap.

Waiting Has a Cost

Delaying planning can reduce options. It may leave less time to reposition assets, evaluate coverage, or coordinate income decisions before pressure arrives.

Waiting to plan can narrow choices. Some insurance options depend on health, some repositioning strategies require time, and some family conversations are easier before a crisis creates urgency.

In a review, this part of the roadmap is connected back to the household's income needs, tax picture, risk comfort, liquidity,

spouse protection, and future flexibility. The goal is to understand how waiting has a cost affects the broader plan before a decision is made.

The important issue is connection. A decision that seems small by itself can affect income, taxes, risk, spouse protection, healthcare flexibility, or future choices.

A better approach is to bring the question into the open. A review can sort what is clear, what needs confirmation, and what should be coordinated with another qualified professional.

The useful planning move is to connect the topic to real household cash flow. If the decision changes monthly income, liquidity, taxes, spouse protection, healthcare flexibility, or legacy intentions, it deserves a place on the roadmap.

A Client-Style Example

Marie thinks a comfortable starting income is enough until she imagines groceries, insurance, taxes, and repairs increasing over twenty-five years.

Marie starts with today's comfort level, then tests what happens if costs rise gradually. The exercise does not predict the future, but it shows why some income may need room to grow.

The lesson is not that every reader with a similar story needs the same answer. The lesson is that personal context changes the planning conversation.

If a scenario feels familiar, it is worth writing down what part caught your attention and bringing that note to a review.

Common Misunderstandings

Inflation is not only a headline number; it is a household experience.

Longevity planning is not pessimistic. It is preparation for the retirement many people hope to have.

A third misunderstanding is assuming the chapter topic can be decided by a rule of thumb. A rule of thumb may start a conversation, but it cannot replace a review of income need, time horizon, health, family priorities, tax status, and comfort with tradeoffs.

What People Often Overlook

Home maintenance, insurance, and taxes can rise even when a mortgage is gone.

A long retirement may include several different spending seasons.

People also overlook how this issue interacts with the rest of the plan. Home maintenance, insurance, and taxes can rise even when a mortgage is gone.

People also overlook how this issue interacts with the rest of the plan. A long retirement may include several different spending seasons.

What a Planning Review Usually Looks At

A review for this topic usually focuses on the facts that affect the household's next decision:

current and future income sources, including Social Security, pension income, employment income, annuity income, and portfolio withdrawals

essential expenses, lifestyle expenses, healthcare costs, debt payments, family support, charitable goals, and emergency reserves

account types, tax treatment, beneficiary designations, liquidity needs, market exposure, and protection strategies

insurance coverage, life insurance, long-term care concerns, Medicare planning, survivor income needs, and legacy intentions

The review should connect decisions rather than treating each topic as a separate island.

If inflation or longevity worries you, use https://host.safemsngr.com/widget/bookings/psglifeandretirementplan to review how your income plan may need to adapt.

Questions to Bring Into the Conversation

Use these questions as conversation starters for your own situation:

What if one or both of us live much longer than expected?

How might rising costs affect the income that feels comfortable today?

Which decisions become harder if we wait several more years to review them?

They are not do-it-yourself instructions; they are prompts to bring into a qualified review.

A Calm Planning Note

Inflation and longevity do not require fear, but they do require room in the plan for costs and needs to change.

A calm planning conversation should make the next step feel clearer. It may lead to action, or it may simply identify what should be watched, verified, or discussed with a tax, legal, Medicare, Social Security, or insurance professional.

The Retirement That Lasts Longer Than the Budget

Longevity changes the retirement income question. A five-year plan may look easy. A twenty-five- or thirty-year retirement asks more from the money. It asks whether income can adapt, whether healthcare costs can be absorbed, whether the home can be maintained, and whether a surviving spouse can continue with dignity.

Inflation adds pressure because it does not require a crisis to matter. Small increases repeated over many years can change the feel of a budget. A retiree may not notice one increase in groceries or insurance, but the combined effect can reduce flexibility over time.

This is why a roadmap should include both stable income and adaptable resources. Some dollars may need protection. Some may need growth potential. Some should remain accessible. The right mix depends on the household's time horizon and comfort with tradeoffs.

Chapter Summary

This chapter's key point is that inflation, longevity, and the cost of waiting should be reviewed in context, not as an isolated decision.

The reader does not need to leave with a product decision. The better goal is to leave with clearer questions and a stronger understanding of what personal review should cover.

Next, safe money strategies are explained in plain language.

Chapter 8: Safe Money Strategies Explained Simply

Safe money strategies are often discussed emotionally, but they deserve a calm explanation.

Safe money generally means money protected from direct market loss, though protection, growth potential, liquidity, and guarantees all involve tradeoffs.

Protection Has a Purpose

Safe money is not about fear. It is about assigning some dollars to stability so the overall plan is not forced to depend on market performance at the wrong time.

Safe money is best understood by job description. These are dollars intended to avoid direct market loss, support predictable income, preserve principal under stated contract rules, or create emotional breathing room when other assets move up and down.

In a review, this part of the roadmap is connected back to the household's income needs, tax picture, risk comfort, liquidity, spouse protection, and future flexibility. The goal is to understand how protection has a purpose affects the broader plan before a decision is made.

For safe money, the important issue is tradeoff. Protection from direct market loss can be valuable, but it should be weighed against liquidity needs, growth potential, and contract terms.

A better approach is to bring the question into the open. A review can sort what is clear, what needs confirmation, and what should be coordinated with another qualified professional.

The useful planning move is to connect the topic to real household cash flow. If the decision changes monthly income, liquidity, taxes, spouse protection, healthcare flexibility, or legacy intentions, it deserves a place on the roadmap.

Safe Does Not Mean Magic

Protection from direct market loss can come with limits, lower liquidity, surrender charges, caps, participation rates, fees, or other rules depending on the strategy.

Protection is not the same as perfection. A bank account, fixed annuity, fixed indexed annuity, Treasury security, or other conservative tool may each offer a different mix of access, rate certainty, tax treatment, liquidity, guarantees, and limitations.

In a review, this part of the roadmap is connected back to the household's income needs, tax picture, risk comfort, liquidity, spouse protection, and future flexibility. The goal is to understand how safe does not mean magic affects the broader plan before a decision is made.

For safe money, the important issue is tradeoff. Protection from direct market loss can be valuable, but it should be weighed against liquidity needs, growth potential, and contract terms.

A better approach is to bring the question into the open. A review can sort what is clear, what needs confirmation, and what should be coordinated with another qualified professional.

The useful planning move is to connect the topic to real household cash flow. If the decision changes monthly income, liquidity, taxes, spouse protection, healthcare flexibility, or legacy intentions, it deserves a place on the roadmap.

The Right Amount Is Personal

Some households need more protected income than others. The amount depends on expenses, guaranteed income, emergency reserves, risk tolerance, health, and family priorities.

The planning question is how much safety is enough. Too little protection may leave a retiree exposed during downturns. Too much may limit flexibility, growth potential, or access. The right balance depends on the household.

In a review, this part of the roadmap is connected back to the household's income needs, tax picture, risk comfort, liquidity, spouse protection, and future flexibility. The goal is to understand how the right amount is personal affects the broader plan before a decision is made.

For safe money, the important issue is tradeoff. Protection from direct market loss can be valuable, but it should be weighed against liquidity needs, growth potential, and contract terms.

A better approach is to bring the question into the open. A review can sort what is clear, what needs confirmation, and what should be coordinated with another qualified professional.

The useful planning move is to connect the topic to real household cash flow. If the decision changes monthly income, liquidity, taxes, spouse protection, healthcare flexibility, or legacy intentions, it deserves a place on the roadmap.

A Client-Style Example

Gerald wants every dollar safe, but his review shows that some money may need liquidity, some may need growth potential, and some may need income protection.

Gerald's concern about safety is valid, but the review also protects his flexibility. Some money can be positioned conservatively while enough remains accessible for repairs, travel, and unexpected family needs.

The lesson is not that every reader with a similar story needs the same answer. The lesson is that personal context changes the planning conversation.

If a scenario feels familiar, it is worth writing down what part caught your attention and bringing that note to a review.

Common Misunderstandings

Protected does not mean unrestricted.

Safe money can reduce one risk while introducing tradeoffs such as lower upside or limited liquidity.

A third misunderstanding is assuming the chapter topic can be decided by a rule of thumb. A rule of thumb may start a conversation, but it cannot replace a review of income need, time horizon, health, family priorities, tax status, and comfort with tradeoffs.

People sometimes hear the phrase safe money and assume there are no tradeoffs. A protected strategy may still involve surrender charges, limits on access, fees, or lower upside.

What People Often Overlook

Liquidity needs should be protected before money is committed to longer-term contracts.

Carrier strength and contract terms matter when guarantees are discussed.

People also overlook how this issue interacts with the rest of the plan. Liquidity needs should be protected before money is committed to longer-term contracts.

People also overlook how this issue interacts with the rest of the plan. Carrier strength and contract terms matter when guarantees are discussed.

What a Planning Review Usually Looks At

A safe-money review compares protection with access and flexibility:

current and future income sources, including Social Security, pension income, employment income, annuity income, and portfolio withdrawals

essential expenses, lifestyle expenses, healthcare costs, debt payments, family support, charitable goals, and emergency reserves

account types, tax treatment, beneficiary designations, liquidity needs, market exposure, and protection strategies

insurance coverage, life insurance, long-term care concerns, Medicare planning, survivor income needs, and legacy intentions

For safe money strategies, the review may examine how much income should be protected from direct market loss and how much liquidity should remain outside contracts.

If you want to understand what should be protected and what should stay flexible, a review can help: https://host.safemsngr.com/widget/bookings/psglifeandretirementplan.

Questions to Bring Into the Conversation

Use these questions to compare protection, access, and contract rules:

How much income do we want protected from direct market loss?

What liquidity would we give up in exchange for protection or contract benefits?

Which dollars should stay flexible outside any long-term contract?

They are not do-it-yourself instructions; they are prompts to bring into a qualified review.

A Calm Planning Note

Safe money strategies can bring comfort, but comfort should still be reviewed carefully. A protected strategy should be understood in writing, including what is guaranteed, what is not guaranteed, how access works, and what costs or limitations may apply.

A calm planning conversation should make the next step feel clearer. It may lead to action, or it may simply identify what should be watched, verified, or discussed with a tax, legal, Medicare, Social Security, or insurance professional.

The Tradeoff Behind Safety

Safe money conversations should be honest. Protection has value, but protection usually comes with a tradeoff. A bank account may offer access but limited growth. A fixed annuity may offer a declared rate and protection from direct market loss, but may include surrender charges and carrier-dependent guarantees. A fixed indexed annuity may offer index-linked interest potential with downside protection, but the crediting method can limit upside and change under contract rules.

The question is not whether safety is good or bad. The question is what the household needs safety to accomplish. Some retirees need safety for essential income. Others need it for emotional comfort. Others need it because a spouse would not want to manage market volatility alone. Each reason matters, but each may lead to a different amount of protected money.

A review should also protect liquidity. Safe money should not mean every dollar is locked away. Emergencies, home repairs, healthcare needs, and family situations require accessible funds.

That balance is where suitability lives.

Chapter Summary

This chapter's key point is that safe money strategies explained simply should be reviewed in context, not as an isolated decision.

The reader does not need to leave with a product decision. The better goal is to leave with clearer questions and a stronger understanding of what personal review should cover.

Next, annuities are introduced neutrally so readers can understand the contracts without confusion.

Chapter 9: Annuities Without the Confusion

Annuities are often either oversold or misunderstood, and neither helps consumers make good decisions.

An annuity is a contract with an insurance company, and its value depends on whether its features fit the retiree's needs.

Start With the Contract

An annuity is a contract. That means details matter. The promises, limits, charges, income options, and liquidity provisions are in the contract, not in a general description.

Annuities become confusing when people talk about them as one thing. They are contracts, and contracts have terms. The relevant questions are practical: What does it protect? How does it grow? How can money be accessed? What income can it provide? What does it cost?

In a review, this part of the roadmap is connected back to the household's income needs, tax picture, risk comfort, liquidity, spouse protection, and future flexibility. The goal is to understand how start with the contract affects the broader plan before a decision is made.

For annuities, the important issue is suitability. A contract should be evaluated by what problem it is intended to solve and what restrictions come with its benefits.

A better approach is to bring the question into the open. A review can sort what is clear, what needs confirmation, and what should be coordinated with another qualified professional.

The useful planning move is to connect the topic to real household cash flow. If the decision changes monthly income, liquidity, taxes, spouse protection, healthcare flexibility, or legacy intentions, it deserves a place on the roadmap.

Different Annuities, Different Jobs

Some annuities are designed for accumulation, some for income, some for principal protection, and some for a blend of features. Comparing them requires knowing the job they are meant to do.

A neutral annuity conversation includes pros and cons in the same breath. Potential benefits may include principal protection from direct market loss, tax deferral, income options, or lifetime income features. Tradeoffs may include surrender charges, fees, lower liquidity, limited upside, exclusions, and tax consequences.

In a review, this part of the roadmap is connected back to the household's income needs, tax picture, risk comfort, liquidity, spouse protection, and future flexibility. The goal is to understand how different annuities, different jobs affects the broader plan before a decision is made.

For annuities, the important issue is suitability. A contract should be evaluated by what problem it is intended to solve and what restrictions come with its benefits.

A better approach is to bring the question into the open. A review can sort what is clear, what needs confirmation, and what should be coordinated with another qualified professional.

The useful planning move is to connect the topic to real household cash flow. If the decision changes monthly income, liquidity, taxes, spouse protection, healthcare flexibility, or legacy intentions, it deserves a place on the roadmap.

Suitability Comes First

An annuity may be useful for one household and inappropriate for another. A careful review should consider liquidity, income need, time horizon, tax status, health, beneficiaries, and comfort with contract restrictions.

No annuity should be treated as right for everyone. Suitability depends on income need, time horizon, liquidity, health, beneficiaries, existing assets, tax status, and comfort with contract restrictions.

In a review, this part of the roadmap is connected back to the household's income needs, tax picture, risk comfort, liquidity, spouse protection, and future flexibility. The goal is to understand how suitability comes first affects the broader plan before a decision is made.

For annuities, the important issue is suitability. A contract should be evaluated by what problem it is intended to solve and what restrictions come with its benefits.

A better approach is to bring the question into the open. A review can sort what is clear, what needs confirmation, and what should be coordinated with another qualified professional.

The useful planning move is to connect the topic to real household cash flow. If the decision changes monthly income, liquidity, taxes, spouse protection, healthcare flexibility, or legacy intentions, it deserves a place on the roadmap.

A Client-Style Example

Pat hears the word annuity and thinks all annuities are the same, then learns that contract type, surrender period, income options, and fees can vary widely.

Pat's most useful discovery is that an annuity is not a slogan. It is a contract. The review slows down long enough to read what is guaranteed, what is limited, and what depends on the carrier.

The lesson is not that every reader with a similar story needs the same answer. The lesson is that personal context changes the planning conversation.

If a scenario feels familiar, it is worth writing down what part caught your attention and bringing that note to a review.

Common Misunderstandings

All annuities are not alike.

An attractive feature should always be read alongside surrender charges, fees, liquidity limits, and tax treatment.

A third misunderstanding is assuming the chapter topic can be decided by a rule of thumb. A rule of thumb may start a conversation, but it cannot replace a review of income need, time horizon, health, family priorities, tax status, and comfort with tradeoffs.

People often speak about annuities as if they are all identical. The contract type, carrier, surrender period, income option, rider, and tax treatment can make a major difference.

What People Often Overlook

Surrender periods and free-withdrawal provisions should be understood before purchase.

Beneficiary and tax rules can affect how the contract works for a family.

People also overlook how this issue interacts with the rest of the plan. Surrender periods and free-withdrawal provisions should be understood before purchase.

People also overlook how this issue interacts with the rest of the plan. Beneficiary and tax rules can affect how the contract works for a family.

What a Planning Review Usually Looks At

An annuity review should slow down and read the contract features carefully:

current and future income sources, including Social Security, pension income, employment income, annuity income, and portfolio withdrawals

essential expenses, lifestyle expenses, healthcare costs, debt payments, family support, charitable goals, and emergency reserves

account types, tax treatment, beneficiary designations, liquidity needs, market exposure, and protection strategies

insurance coverage, life insurance, long-term care concerns, Medicare planning, survivor income needs, and legacy intentions

For annuities, the review may compare contract purpose, surrender period, fees, riders, income options, tax treatment, and carrier strength.

If an annuity has been suggested to you, review the contract and suitability questions before deciding. You can request that conversation at https://host.safemsngr.com/widget/bookings/psglifeandretirementplan.

Questions to Bring Into the Conversation

Use these questions before treating any annuity feature as a fit:

What problem would an annuity be intended to solve in our plan?

Do we understand the surrender period, fees, liquidity rules, and tax treatment?

How would the contract help or limit a surviving spouse or beneficiaries?

They are not do-it-yourself instructions; they are prompts to bring into a qualified review.

A Calm Planning Note

An annuity conversation should be slow enough for real understanding. If a feature sounds attractive, the next question should be how it works, what it costs, what it limits, and what happens if life does not unfold as expected.

A calm planning conversation should make the next step feel clearer. It may lead to action, or it may simply identify what should be watched, verified, or discussed with a tax, legal, Medicare, Social Security, or insurance professional.

How to Read an Annuity Conversation

When annuities come up, the reader should listen for both benefits and limits. If the conversation only mentions guarantees, it is incomplete. If it only mentions drawbacks, it is also incomplete. A balanced explanation should describe what the contract may do, what it may cost, what it may restrict, and what must be true for the strategy to fit.

The reader should ask whether the annuity is being considered for income, principal protection, tax deferral, legacy planning, long-term care positioning, or another purpose. A contract designed for one job may be disappointing if it is expected to do another. For example, a contract that supports future income may not be ideal for money that could be needed next year.

Suitability is the center of the conversation. Age, state, assets, liquidity, income need, tax status, health, beneficiary goals, and existing coverage all matter.

Chapter Summary

This chapter's key point is that annuities without the confusion should be reviewed in context, not as an isolated decision.

The reader does not need to leave with a product decision. The better goal is to leave with clearer questions and a stronger understanding of what personal review should cover.

Next, the book compares fixed annuities, indexed annuities, and income riders more closely.

Chapter 10: Fixed Annuities, Indexed Annuities, and Income Riders

Different annuity designs solve different problems, and the details matter.

Fixed annuities, fixed indexed annuities, and income riders each have tradeoffs involving rate certainty, index-linked interest, lifetime income, fees, liquidity, and contract rules.

Fixed Annuities in Plain Language

A fixed annuity generally credits interest according to the terms of the contract. It may appeal to someone seeking a declared rate and protection from direct market loss, subject to carrier strength and contract rules.

A fixed annuity generally emphasizes a stated interest approach under the contract. A fixed indexed annuity credits interest using an index-linked formula, but the owner is not directly invested in the market index. An income rider may calculate a future income benefit, often for an additional cost.

In a review, this part of the roadmap is connected back to the household's income needs, tax picture, risk comfort, liquidity, spouse protection, and future flexibility. The goal is to understand how fixed annuities in plain language affects the broader plan before a decision is made.

For annuity types, the important issue is detail. Similar names can hide different crediting methods, rider costs, surrender schedules, income rules, and liquidity provisions.

A better approach is to bring the question into the open. A review can sort what is clear, what needs confirmation, and what should be coordinated with another qualified professional.

The useful planning move is to connect the topic to real household cash flow. If the decision changes monthly income, liquidity, taxes, spouse protection, healthcare flexibility, or legacy intentions, it deserves a place on the roadmap.

Indexed Annuities in Plain Language

A fixed indexed annuity credits interest based in part on the movement of an external index, using formulas such as caps, spreads, or participation rates. The owner is not directly invested in the index.

The confusing part is that the most attractive-looking number may not be the cash value. Some riders use a benefit base to calculate income. That base may grow under a formula, but it may not be available as a lump-sum withdrawal.

In a review, this part of the roadmap is connected back to the household's income needs, tax picture, risk comfort, liquidity, spouse protection, and future flexibility. The goal is to understand how indexed annuities in plain language affects the broader plan before a decision is made.

For annuity types, the important issue is detail. Similar names can hide different crediting methods, rider costs, surrender schedules, income rules, and liquidity provisions.

A better approach is to bring the question into the open. A review can sort what is clear, what needs confirmation, and what should be coordinated with another qualified professional.

The useful planning move is to connect the topic to real household cash flow. If the decision changes monthly income, liquidity, taxes, spouse protection, healthcare flexibility, or legacy intentions, it deserves a place on the roadmap.

Income Riders Need Careful Review

An income rider may provide a way to calculate future income, often for an additional cost. The benefit base used for income is not always the same as cash value, so explanation matters.

A careful review compares surrender schedules, free-withdrawal provisions, rider charges, caps, spreads, participation rates, renewal discretion, death benefit rules, taxation, and carrier financial strength.

In a review, this part of the roadmap is connected back to the household's income needs, tax picture, risk comfort, liquidity, spouse protection, and future flexibility. The goal is to understand how income riders need careful review affects the broader plan before a decision is made.

For annuity types, the important issue is detail. Similar names can hide different crediting methods, rider costs, surrender schedules, income rules, and liquidity provisions.

A better approach is to bring the question into the open. A review can sort what is clear, what needs confirmation, and what should be coordinated with another qualified professional.

The useful planning move is to connect the topic to real household cash flow. If the decision changes monthly income, liquidity, taxes, spouse protection, healthcare flexibility, or legacy intentions, it deserves a place on the roadmap.

A Client-Style Example

Nora compares two contracts with similar names and realizes one focuses on declared interest while the other focuses on a future income benefit.

Nora learns to compare the job of each contract. One option may focus on stated interest, another on index-linked crediting, and another on future income. Similar brochures do not mean similar outcomes.

The lesson is not that every reader with a similar story needs the same answer. The lesson is that personal context changes the planning conversation.

If a scenario feels familiar, it is worth writing down what part caught your attention and bringing that note to a review.

Common Misunderstandings

A benefit base may not be cash value.

Index-linked interest is not the same as direct stock market investment.

A third misunderstanding is assuming the chapter topic can be decided by a rule of thumb. A rule of thumb may start a conversation, but it cannot replace a review of income need, time horizon, health, family priorities, tax status, and comfort with tradeoffs.

People may confuse an income benefit value with cash value. This is especially important when reviewing riders, because the number used to calculate income may not be withdrawable as a lump sum.

What People Often Overlook

Renewal rates, caps, spreads, and participation rates may change under contract rules.

Rider fees can affect value even when the rider solves a real income concern.

People also overlook how this issue interacts with the rest of the plan. Renewal rates, caps, spreads, and participation rates may change under contract rules.

People also overlook how this issue interacts with the rest of the plan. Rider fees can affect value even when the rider solves a real income concern.

What a Planning Review Usually Looks At

A fixed, indexed, or rider review compares the mechanics rather than the marketing names:

current and future income sources, including Social Security, pension income, employment income, annuity income, and portfolio withdrawals

essential expenses, lifestyle expenses, healthcare costs, debt payments, family support, charitable goals, and emergency reserves

account types, tax treatment, beneficiary designations, liquidity needs, market exposure, and protection strategies

insurance coverage, life insurance, long-term care concerns, Medicare planning, survivor income needs, and legacy intentions

For fixed and indexed annuities, the review may distinguish declared rates, index-linked crediting methods, income rider calculations, and cash value access.

If fixed, indexed, or rider language feels unclear, bring the contract details to a review at https://host.safemsngr.com/widget/bookings/psglifeandretirementplan.

Questions to Bring Into the Conversation

Use these questions when comparing annuity designs:

Are we comparing fixed annuities, indexed annuities, and income riders accurately?

Do we know the difference between cash value and any income benefit value?

What happens if we need more access to the money than expected?

They are not do-it-yourself instructions; they are prompts to bring into a qualified review.

A Calm Planning Note

When comparing annuity types, similar words can create confusion. A review should translate contract language into practical questions: What can I access? What income can I receive? What can change? What is tied to carrier claims-paying ability?

A calm planning conversation should make the next step feel clearer. It may lead to action, or it may simply identify what should be watched, verified, or discussed with a tax, legal, Medicare, Social Security, or insurance professional.

Comparing Features Without Getting Lost

Fixed annuities, fixed indexed annuities, and income riders can sound similar because they all live under the annuity umbrella. The details separate them. A fixed annuity may be easier to understand because the interest approach is usually stated more directly. A fixed indexed annuity may require more explanation because interest credits depend on formulas tied to an index. An income rider may require a separate explanation because the rider's income calculation may not equal cash value.

A careful review should translate each feature into a household question. How much can be accessed without penalty? How long does the surrender period last? What fees apply? What happens at death? What changes after the first contract year? How is income calculated? Which guarantees depend on the issuing carrier?

The goal is not to make the reader suspicious. The goal is to make the contract understandable enough for an informed review.

When the language becomes clear, the reader can compare choices with less pressure and fewer assumptions.

Chapter Summary

This chapter's key point is that fixed annuities, indexed annuities, and income riders should be reviewed in context, not as an isolated decision.

The reader does not need to leave with a product decision. The better goal is to leave with clearer questions and a stronger understanding of what personal review should cover.

Next, the roadmap turns to spouse and survivor income protection.

Chapter 11: Protecting a Spouse or Survivor

A retirement income plan should be able to answer what happens when life changes for one spouse.

Survivor planning looks at income reductions, tax filing changes, household expenses, account access, beneficiary designations, and emotional simplicity.

One Plan, Two Lives

For couples, retirement income planning should consider both lives. The plan should not only work while both spouses are living and able to manage details.

A retirement plan should be tested for the day one spouse is managing alone. Income may change, taxes may change, paperwork may become harder, and the surviving spouse may still face many of the same household expenses.

In a review, this part of the roadmap is connected back to the household's income needs, tax picture, risk comfort, liquidity, spouse protection, and future flexibility. The goal is to understand how one plan, two lives affects the broader plan before a decision is made.

The important issue is connection. A decision that seems small by itself can affect income, taxes, risk, spouse protection, healthcare flexibility, or future choices.

A better approach is to bring the question into the open. A review can sort what is clear, what needs confirmation, and what should be coordinated with another qualified professional.

The useful planning move is to connect the topic to real household cash flow. If the decision changes monthly income, liquidity, taxes, spouse protection, healthcare flexibility, or legacy intentions, it deserves a place on the roadmap.

Income Can Change Quickly

A survivor may lose one Social Security benefit, may face different tax brackets, may lose pension income depending on elections, and may still have many of the same household expenses.

Survivor planning is not only about insurance. It includes pension elections, Social Security timing, beneficiary designations, account ownership, passwords, bill-pay systems, emergency reserves, and whether the surviving spouse knows who to call.

In a review, this part of the roadmap is connected back to the household's income needs, tax picture, risk comfort, liquidity, spouse protection, and future flexibility. The goal is to understand how income can change quickly affects the broader plan before a decision is made.

The important issue is connection. A decision that seems small by itself can affect income, taxes, risk, spouse protection, healthcare flexibility, or future choices.

A better approach is to bring the question into the open. A review can sort what is clear, what needs confirmation, and what should be coordinated with another qualified professional.

The useful planning move is to connect the topic to real household cash flow. If the decision changes monthly income, liquidity, taxes, spouse protection, healthcare flexibility, or legacy intentions, it deserves a place on the roadmap.

Simplicity Is a Gift

A plan that is organized, documented, and reviewed can be a practical act of care for the person who may one day have to manage alone.

The goal is not to make a difficult life event easy. The goal is to reduce avoidable confusion and protect income when the household is least interested in sorting through financial details.

In a review, this part of the roadmap is connected back to the household's income needs, tax picture, risk comfort, liquidity,

spouse protection, and future flexibility. The goal is to understand how simplicity is a gift affects the broader plan before a decision is made.

The important issue is connection. A decision that seems small by itself can affect income, taxes, risk, spouse protection, healthcare flexibility, or future choices.

A better approach is to bring the question into the open. A review can sort what is clear, what needs confirmation, and what should be coordinated with another qualified professional.

The useful planning move is to connect the topic to real household cash flow. If the decision changes monthly income, liquidity, taxes, spouse protection, healthcare flexibility, or legacy intentions, it deserves a place on the roadmap.

A Client-Style Example

After a friend's spouse dies, Thomas and Angela realize they have never looked at their own income plan from the survivor's point of view.

Thomas and Angela review what each spouse would actually receive if the other died first. The exercise is emotional, but it turns vague concern into specific planning steps.

The lesson is not that every reader with a similar story needs the same answer. The lesson is that personal context changes the planning conversation.

If a scenario feels familiar, it is worth writing down what part caught your attention and bringing that note to a review.

Common Misunderstandings

Couples sometimes assume the surviving spouse will simply continue the same plan.

A beneficiary form is not a substitute for a coordinated survivor income review.

A third misunderstanding is assuming the chapter topic can be decided by a rule of thumb. A rule of thumb may start a conversation, but it cannot replace a review of income need, time horizon, health, family priorities, tax status, and comfort with tradeoffs.

What People Often Overlook

Tax filing status may change after the first death.

The survivor may need simpler account access and fewer moving pieces.

People also overlook how this issue interacts with the rest of the plan. Tax filing status may change after the first death.

People also overlook how this issue interacts with the rest of the plan. The survivor may need simpler account access and fewer moving pieces.

What a Planning Review Usually Looks At

A survivor review looks at the household after the first death:

current and future income sources, including Social Security, pension income, employment income, annuity income, and portfolio withdrawals

essential expenses, lifestyle expenses, healthcare costs, debt payments, family support, charitable goals, and emergency reserves

account types, tax treatment, beneficiary designations, liquidity needs, market exposure, and protection strategies

insurance coverage, life insurance, long-term care concerns, Medicare planning, survivor income needs, and legacy intentions

The review should connect decisions rather than treating each topic as a separate island.

If a surviving spouse would need a clearer plan, schedule time to review the income picture at https://host.safemsngr.com/widget/bookings/psglifeandretirementplan.

Questions to Bring Into the Conversation

Use these questions to look at the plan from the survivor's chair:

What income remains when the first spouse dies?

Will the surviving spouse understand where accounts, policies, passwords, and documents are located?

Are beneficiary designations and ownership arrangements current?

They are not do-it-yourself instructions; they are prompts to bring into a qualified review.

A Calm Planning Note

Survivor planning is an act of care. It can feel uncomfortable to discuss, but it often brings relief because both spouses can see what would happen and what might need to be simplified.

A calm planning conversation should make the next step feel clearer. It may lead to action, or it may simply identify what should be watched, verified, or discussed with a tax, legal, Medicare, Social Security, or insurance professional.

Looking Through the Survivor's Eyes

A survivor income review often reveals issues that were easy to miss while both spouses were living. One Social Security benefit may disappear. A pension may continue, reduce, or stop depending on the election chosen. Required income may not fall as much as expected because housing, utilities, insurance, taxes, and transportation may remain similar.

The surviving spouse may also have a different comfort level with financial decisions. One spouse may have handled investments, insurance, taxes, and bill pay for decades. If that spouse dies first, the plan may suddenly become both financial and administrative. Simplicity can be a form of protection.

Couples do not need to make the conversation gloomy. They can treat it as an act of care: organize documents, review beneficiaries, discuss income, and make sure the survivor knows who to call.

Chapter Summary

This chapter's key point is that protecting a spouse or survivor should be reviewed in context, not as an isolated decision.

The reader does not need to leave with a product decision. The better goal is to leave with clearer questions and a stronger understanding of what personal review should cover.

Next, long-term care is addressed as a possible income gap.

Chapter 12: Long-Term Care and Retirement Income Gaps

Long-term care needs can turn a workable retirement income plan into a stressed one if they are ignored.

Planning for care means considering who would provide help, how costs could be paid, and what assets or income would be exposed.

Care Is a Cash Flow Issue

Long-term care is often discussed as a healthcare issue, but it is also a retirement income issue. Paying for care can redirect income and assets away from the original plan.

Long-term care can create an income gap because the need is often ongoing. Help with bathing, dressing, transferring, meals, memory care, home care, assisted living, or nursing care can redirect income away from the original retirement lifestyle.

In a review, this part of the roadmap is connected back to the household's income needs, tax picture, risk comfort, liquidity, spouse protection, and future flexibility. The goal is to understand how care is a cash flow issue affects the broader plan before a decision is made.

For long-term care, the important issue is impact. Care costs can affect the person receiving care, the spouse at home, adult children, and legacy intentions.

A better approach is to bring the question into the open. A review can sort what is clear, what needs confirmation, and what should be coordinated with another qualified professional.

The useful planning move is to connect the topic to real household cash flow. If the decision changes monthly income, liquidity, taxes, spouse protection, healthcare flexibility, or legacy intentions, it deserves a place on the roadmap.

Family Care Has Costs Too

Even when family members provide help, there can be lost wages, travel costs, home modifications, emotional strain, and coordination challenges.

Many families assume care will be handled informally. Sometimes it is, but family care still has costs: time away from work, travel, home modifications, emotional strain, and coordination. Planning should not pretend those costs are invisible.

In a review, this part of the roadmap is connected back to the household's income needs, tax picture, risk comfort, liquidity, spouse protection, and future flexibility. The goal is to understand how family care has costs too affects the broader plan before a decision is made.

For long-term care, the important issue is impact. Care costs can affect the person receiving care, the spouse at home, adult children, and legacy intentions.

A better approach is to bring the question into the open. A review can sort what is clear, what needs confirmation, and what should be coordinated with another qualified professional.

The useful planning move is to connect the topic to real household cash flow. If the decision changes monthly income, liquidity, taxes, spouse protection, healthcare flexibility, or legacy intentions, it deserves a place on the roadmap.

Options Are Better Before Crisis

Planning before care is needed usually leaves more room to evaluate insurance, asset positioning, family roles, and legal documents.

A review may compare self-funding, traditional long-term care insurance, hybrid life or annuity-based designs, Medicaid considerations, legal planning, and the income needs of a spouse who remains at home.

In a review, this part of the roadmap is connected back to the household's income needs, tax picture, risk comfort, liquidity, spouse protection, and future flexibility. The goal is to understand how options are better before crisis affects the broader plan before a decision is made.

For long-term care, the important issue is impact. Care costs can affect the person receiving care, the spouse at home, adult children, and legacy intentions.

A better approach is to bring the question into the open. A review can sort what is clear, what needs confirmation, and what should be coordinated with another qualified professional.

The useful planning move is to connect the topic to real household cash flow. If the decision changes monthly income, liquidity, taxes, spouse protection, healthcare flexibility, or legacy intentions, it deserves a place on the roadmap.

A Client-Style Example

Ben assumes Medicare will cover extended care, then learns that custodial care and long-term support require a separate conversation.

Ben's assumption about Medicare changes once care needs are described plainly. The review helps him think through home care, family help, insurance options, and how a spouse's income would be protected.

The lesson is not that every reader with a similar story needs the same answer. The lesson is that personal context changes the planning conversation.

If a scenario feels familiar, it is worth writing down what part caught your attention and bringing that note to a review.

Common Misunderstandings

Medicare is often misunderstood as long-term custodial care coverage.

Family care may feel free, but it can carry real financial and emotional costs.

A third misunderstanding is assuming the chapter topic can be decided by a rule of thumb. A rule of thumb may start a conversation, but it cannot replace a review of income need, time horizon, health, family priorities, tax status, and comfort with tradeoffs.

People often believe Medicare covers most long-term custodial care. That assumption can create a serious planning gap.

What People Often Overlook

The spouse at home has income needs too.

Legal documents should be reviewed before a care crisis.

People also overlook how this issue interacts with the rest of the plan. The spouse at home has income needs too.

People also overlook how this issue interacts with the rest of the plan. Legal documents should be reviewed before a care crisis.

What a Planning Review Usually Looks At

A long-term care review looks at income pressure before a care need appears:

current and future income sources, including Social Security, pension income, employment income, annuity income, and portfolio withdrawals

essential expenses, lifestyle expenses, healthcare costs, debt payments, family support, charitable goals, and emergency reserves

account types, tax treatment, beneficiary designations, liquidity needs, market exposure, and protection strategies

insurance coverage, life insurance, long-term care concerns, Medicare planning, survivor income needs, and legacy intentions

For long-term care, the review may discuss insurance options, self-funding capacity, family support assumptions, and legal documents that should be reviewed by an attorney.

If care costs could pressure your retirement income, bring that concern into a planning conversation at https://host.safemsngr.com/widget/bookings/psglifeandretirementplan.

Questions to Bring Into the Conversation

Use these questions to discuss care needs before they become urgent:

Who would provide care if we needed help with daily activities?

How would care costs affect the spouse who remains at home?

Should we compare insurance, hybrid protection, self-funding, and family-support assumptions?

They are not do-it-yourself instructions; they are prompts to bring into a qualified review.

A Calm Planning Note

Long-term care planning should be handled with dignity. The question is not only how care could be paid for, but how choices could protect independence, reduce family stress, and preserve income for a spouse at home.

A calm planning conversation should make the next step feel clearer. It may lead to action, or it may simply identify what should be watched, verified, or discussed with a tax, legal, Medicare, Social Security, or insurance professional.

Care Costs and the Spouse at Home

Long-term care planning should consider two people when a couple is involved: the person receiving care and the spouse who remains at home. A care need can redirect income toward aides, facilities, home modifications, transportation, medication management, or family support. Meanwhile, the spouse at home still needs groceries, housing, utilities, transportation, insurance, and a life that remains livable.

This is where planning can protect dignity. The conversation may include insurance, hybrid policies, asset positioning, family care expectations, legal documents, and Medicaid-related questions for qualified professionals. Not every household will choose insurance. Not every household can qualify. But every household benefits from understanding the possible income gap.

Ignoring long-term care does not make the risk disappear. It simply leaves the family to solve it under pressure later.

Chapter Summary

This chapter's key point is that long-term care and retirement income gaps should be reviewed in context, not as an isolated decision.

The reader does not need to leave with a product decision. The better goal is to leave with clearer questions and a stronger understanding of what personal review should cover.

Next, life insurance and legacy planning are placed inside the broader protection conversation.

Chapter 13: Life Insurance, Legacy, and Protection Planning

Protection planning is not only about death benefits; it is about promises, people, and unfinished responsibilities.

Life insurance and legacy planning may support spouse protection, family goals, debt concerns, charitable intentions, business continuity, or tax-aware transfer strategies.

Legacy Starts With the Living Plan

A legacy goal should not quietly weaken the retiree's own income security. The first question is usually whether the retirement plan works for the person who owns it.

Legacy planning begins with the living client. It is generous to want to leave money to children, grandchildren, a church, or a cause, but the first promise is usually that the retiree can live with dignity and enough flexibility.

In a review, this part of the roadmap is connected back to the household's income needs, tax picture, risk comfort, liquidity, spouse protection, and future flexibility. The goal is to understand how legacy starts with the living plan affects the broader plan before a decision is made.

For legacy planning, the important issue is order. Protecting the retiree's income comes first, then the plan can consider how assets may pass to others.

A better approach is to bring the question into the open. A review can sort what is clear, what needs confirmation, and what should be coordinated with another qualified professional.

The useful planning move is to connect the topic to real household cash flow. If the decision changes monthly income, liquidity, taxes, spouse protection, healthcare flexibility, or legacy intentions, it deserves a place on the roadmap.

Protection Can Serve Many Purposes

Life insurance may support income replacement, debt payoff, estate liquidity, charitable wishes, family equalization, or business needs, depending on suitability and underwriting.

Life insurance may help some families transfer wealth, replace income, pay final expenses, support business continuity, equalize inheritances, or provide liquidity. It may not fit every budget, health situation, or objective.

In a review, this part of the roadmap is connected back to the household's income needs, tax picture, risk comfort, liquidity, spouse protection, and future flexibility. The goal is to understand how protection can serve many purposes affects the broader plan before a decision is made.

For legacy planning, the important issue is order. Protecting the retiree's income comes first, then the plan can consider how assets may pass to others.

A better approach is to bring the question into the open. A review can sort what is clear, what needs confirmation, and what should be coordinated with another qualified professional.

The useful planning move is to connect the topic to real household cash flow. If the decision changes monthly income, liquidity, taxes, spouse protection, healthcare flexibility, or legacy intentions, it deserves a place on the roadmap.

Beneficiaries Need Attention

Beneficiary designations can override intentions in a will. A review should check whether names, percentages, contingent beneficiaries, and ownership arrangements still match the plan.

Beneficiary forms deserve more attention than they usually receive. A will may express intentions, but account and policy beneficiary designations often control where assets go. Old names, missing contingents, or mismatched percentages can create preventable problems.

In a review, this part of the roadmap is connected back to the household's income needs, tax picture, risk comfort, liquidity, spouse protection, and future flexibility. The goal is to understand how beneficiaries need attention affects the broader plan before a decision is made.

For legacy planning, the important issue is order. Protecting the retiree's income comes first, then the plan can consider how assets may pass to others.

A better approach is to bring the question into the open. A review can sort what is clear, what needs confirmation, and what should be coordinated with another qualified professional.

The useful planning move is to connect the topic to real household cash flow. If the decision changes monthly income, liquidity, taxes, spouse protection, healthcare flexibility, or legacy intentions, it deserves a place on the roadmap.

A Client-Style Example

Janet wants to leave something for children, but she also needs to preserve enough income and emergency flexibility for herself.

Janet's legacy goal remains important, but it is placed after her income and care needs. That order allows generosity without quietly creating pressure for her future self.

The lesson is not that every reader with a similar story needs the same answer. The lesson is that personal context changes the planning conversation.

If a scenario feels familiar, it is worth writing down what part caught your attention and bringing that note to a review.

Common Misunderstandings

Legacy planning is not only for wealthy families.

A legacy goal should not quietly weaken the retiree's own income security.

A third misunderstanding is assuming the chapter topic can be decided by a rule of thumb. A rule of thumb may start a conversation, but it cannot replace a review of income need, time horizon, health, family priorities, tax status, and comfort with tradeoffs.

What People Often Overlook

Beneficiary designations can override intentions.

Equal is not always the same as fair when family circumstances differ.

People also overlook how this issue interacts with the rest of the plan. Beneficiary designations can override intentions.

People also overlook how this issue interacts with the rest of the plan. Equal is not always the same as fair when family circumstances differ.

What a Planning Review Usually Looks At

A legacy review checks whether intentions, documents, and beneficiary records line up:

current and future income sources, including Social Security, pension income, employment income, annuity income, and portfolio withdrawals

essential expenses, lifestyle expenses, healthcare costs, debt payments, family support, charitable goals, and emergency reserves

account types, tax treatment, beneficiary designations, liquidity needs, market exposure, and protection strategies

insurance coverage, life insurance, long-term care concerns, Medicare planning, survivor income needs, and legacy intentions

The review should connect decisions rather than treating each topic as a separate island.

If protection and legacy goals need to be balanced, you can request a review at https://host.safemsngr.com/widget/bookings/psglifeandretirementplan.

Questions to Bring Into the Conversation

Use these questions as conversation starters for your own situation:

What do we want money to accomplish after our lifetime?

Are legacy goals balanced with income, healthcare, and emergency needs?

Do our legal documents and beneficiary designations tell the same story?

They are not do-it-yourself instructions; they are prompts to bring into a qualified review.

A Calm Planning Note

Legacy planning works best when it supports the living plan first. A thoughtful legacy is not only about what is left behind; it is also about making sure promises do not create pressure during retirement.

A calm planning conversation should make the next step feel clearer. It may lead to action, or it may simply identify what should be watched, verified, or discussed with a tax, legal, Medicare, Social Security, or insurance professional.

Protection Before Transfer

Legacy planning can be meaningful, but it should not outrun retirement security. A parent may want to leave money to children, but those same children may prefer that the parent has enough income, care options, and emergency reserves. A healthy legacy conversation starts with protection for the living client.

Life insurance may help in the right circumstances, but it should be reviewed for purpose and affordability. Is it meant to replace income for a spouse, pay final expenses, support a business transition, create estate liquidity, equalize inheritances, or leave a charitable gift? Different purposes may call for different policy designs, and underwriting may affect what is available.

Beneficiary designations should be checked with care. A forgotten former beneficiary, missing contingent beneficiary, or mismatch between documents and account forms can undermine the family's intentions.

Chapter Summary

This chapter's key point is that life insurance, legacy, and protection planning should be reviewed in context, not as an isolated decision.

The reader does not need to leave with a product decision. The better goal is to leave with clearer questions and a stronger understanding of what personal review should cover.

Next, the book reviews common mistakes that can weaken an otherwise thoughtful plan.

Chapter 14: Common Retirement Income Mistakes

Mistakes in retirement income planning often come from reasonable decisions made without the full picture.

Common problems include claiming benefits without context, withdrawing without a sequence, ignoring taxes, underestimating healthcare, and chasing returns with income money.

Reasonable Choices Can Still Collide

Many retirement mistakes are not careless. They happen when decisions are made separately and later collide in taxes, income timing, market exposure, or survivor needs.

Most retirement mistakes begin as understandable shortcuts. A friend mentions a claiming age, a headline creates fear, a high advertised rate catches attention, or a retiree keeps using the same investment mix that worked during accumulation.

In a review, this part of the roadmap is connected back to the household's income needs, tax picture, risk comfort, liquidity, spouse protection, and future flexibility. The goal is to understand how reasonable choices can still collide affects the broader plan before a decision is made.

The important issue is connection. A decision that seems small by itself can affect income, taxes, risk, spouse protection, healthcare flexibility, or future choices.

A better approach is to bring the question into the open. A review can sort what is clear, what needs confirmation, and what should be coordinated with another qualified professional.

The useful planning move is to connect the topic to real household cash flow. If the decision changes monthly income, liquidity, taxes, spouse protection, healthcare flexibility, or legacy intentions, it deserves a place on the roadmap.

Chasing One Perfect Answer

The search for the single best product, age, rate, or withdrawal number can distract from building a coordinated plan.

The problem is not that retirees lack intelligence. The problem is that retirement decisions are connected. A withdrawal can affect taxes. A product can affect liquidity. A benefit election can affect a spouse. A market loss can affect future income.

In a review, this part of the roadmap is connected back to the household's income needs, tax picture, risk comfort, liquidity, spouse protection, and future flexibility. The goal is to understand how chasing one perfect answer affects the broader plan before a decision is made.

The important issue is connection. A decision that seems small by itself can affect income, taxes, risk, spouse protection, healthcare flexibility, or future choices.

A better approach is to bring the question into the open. A review can sort what is clear, what needs confirmation, and what should be coordinated with another qualified professional.

The useful planning move is to connect the topic to real household cash flow. If the decision changes monthly income, liquidity, taxes, spouse protection, healthcare flexibility, or legacy intentions, it deserves a place on the roadmap.

Ignoring Friction

Fees, taxes, penalties, surrender charges, required distributions, and timing rules can all create friction. Planning should look for these before they become surprises.

Good planning looks for friction before it becomes expensive: taxes, surrender charges, required distributions, Medicare premium effects, beneficiary errors, and concentration risk.

In a review, this part of the roadmap is connected back to the household's income needs, tax picture, risk comfort, liquidity, spouse protection, and future flexibility. The goal is to understand

how ignoring friction affects the broader plan before a decision is made.

The important issue is connection. A decision that seems small by itself can affect income, taxes, risk, spouse protection, healthcare flexibility, or future choices.

A better approach is to bring the question into the open. A review can sort what is clear, what needs confirmation, and what should be coordinated with another qualified professional.

The useful planning move is to connect the topic to real household cash flow. If the decision changes monthly income, liquidity, taxes, spouse protection, healthcare flexibility, or legacy intentions, it deserves a place on the roadmap.

A Client-Style Example

A recently retired household changes investments, claims benefits, and starts withdrawals separately, then discovers the decisions should have been coordinated.

The household in this chapter has not done anything foolish. They simply made decisions one at a time. The review helps them see where those decisions now overlap.

The lesson is not that every reader with a similar story needs the same answer. The lesson is that personal context changes the planning conversation.

If a scenario feels familiar, it is worth writing down what part caught your attention and bringing that note to a review.

Common Misunderstandings

A rule of thumb may be useful as a conversation starter, not as a personal recommendation.

One strong product feature cannot fix an uncoordinated plan.

A third misunderstanding is assuming the chapter topic can be decided by a rule of thumb. A rule of thumb may start a conversation, but it cannot replace a review of income need, time horizon, health, family priorities, tax status, and comfort with tradeoffs.

What People Often Overlook

Advertising can make isolated features look more important than fit.

Old assumptions may survive long after life has changed.

People also overlook how this issue interacts with the rest of the plan. Advertising can make isolated features look more important than fit.

People also overlook how this issue interacts with the rest of the plan. Old assumptions may survive long after life has changed.

What a Planning Review Usually Looks At

A review for this topic usually focuses on the facts that affect the household's next decision:

current and future income sources, including Social Security, pension income, employment income, annuity income, and portfolio withdrawals

essential expenses, lifestyle expenses, healthcare costs, debt payments, family support, charitable goals, and emergency reserves

account types, tax treatment, beneficiary designations, liquidity needs, market exposure, and protection strategies

insurance coverage, life insurance, long-term care concerns, Medicare planning, survivor income needs, and legacy intentions

The review should connect decisions rather than treating each topic as a separate island.

If you are unsure whether past decisions still fit, use https://host.safemsngr.com/widget/bookings/psglifeandretirementplan to organize a fresh review.

Questions to Bring Into the Conversation

Use these questions as conversation starters for your own situation:

Which decisions have we been making separately that should be coordinated?

Are we relying on rules of thumb that may not fit our household?

Where could taxes, market timing, fees, or liquidity limits surprise us?

They are not do-it-yourself instructions; they are prompts to bring into a qualified review.

A Calm Planning Note

The best mistake prevention is coordination. A decision that looks fine alone may need adjustment when the whole plan is visible.

A calm planning conversation should make the next step feel clearer. It may lead to action, or it may simply identify what should be watched, verified, or discussed with a tax, legal, Medicare, Social Security, or insurance professional.

Why Mistakes Often Look Reasonable at First

The most common retirement income mistakes rarely look reckless in the moment. Claiming a benefit early may feel practical. Moving money after a market loss may feel protective. Buying a product because the headline feature sounds strong may feel responsible. The problem is that each decision can create side effects when it is not reviewed with the whole plan in mind.

This is why a second set of professional eyes can be valuable. A review can ask what the decision solves, what it may complicate, and whether another option would preserve more flexibility. The goal is not to criticize past choices. The goal is to prevent one reasonable decision from creating an avoidable problem later.

Chapter Summary

This chapter's key point is that common retirement income mistakes should be reviewed in context, not as an isolated decision.

The reader does not need to leave with a product decision. The better goal is to leave with clearer questions and a stronger understanding of what personal review should cover.

Next, readers learn what to gather before a retirement income review.

Chapter 15: What to Gather Before a Retirement Income Review

A better planning conversation starts with better information.

Gathering documents helps an advisor see income sources, account types, obligations, insurance, beneficiary arrangements, healthcare coverage, and family priorities.

Bring the Real Picture

A planning review works better when it reflects real accounts, real income sources, real expenses, and real family concerns.

A review is easier when the documents tell the truth. Current statements show account type, value, ownership, and sometimes fees or surrender details. Benefit estimates show timing choices. Policies show promises, exclusions, premiums, beneficiaries, and contract limits.

In a review, this part of the roadmap is connected back to the household's income needs, tax picture, risk comfort, liquidity, spouse protection, and future flexibility. The goal is to understand how bring the real picture affects the broader plan before a decision is made.

The important issue is connection. A decision that seems small by itself can affect income, taxes, risk, spouse protection, healthcare flexibility, or future choices.

A better approach is to bring the question into the open. A review can sort what is clear, what needs confirmation, and what should be coordinated with another qualified professional.

The useful planning move is to connect the topic to real household cash flow. If the decision changes monthly income, liquidity, taxes, spouse protection, healthcare flexibility, or legacy intentions, it deserves a place on the roadmap.

Documents Tell a Story

Statements and policies are not just paperwork. They reveal account types, beneficiaries, rates, guarantees, fees, tax treatment, and deadlines.

Preparation is not about impressing the advisor. It is about preventing guesswork. A missing pension election, old beneficiary form, or unknown annuity surrender period can change the conversation.

In a review, this part of the roadmap is connected back to the household's income needs, tax picture, risk comfort, liquidity, spouse protection, and future flexibility. The goal is to understand how documents tell a story affects the broader plan before a decision is made.

The important issue is connection. A decision that seems small by itself can affect income, taxes, risk, spouse protection, healthcare flexibility, or future choices.

A better approach is to bring the question into the open. A review can sort what is clear, what needs confirmation, and what should be coordinated with another qualified professional.

The useful planning move is to connect the topic to real household cash flow. If the decision changes monthly income, liquidity, taxes, spouse protection, healthcare flexibility, or legacy intentions, it deserves a place on the roadmap.

Questions Are Welcome

The best review is not a test. It is a conversation. Bringing questions helps the professional understand what matters most to you.

Readers should also bring the human details: worries about a spouse, a desire to help children, concern about care costs, charitable goals, debt stress, or discomfort with market swings.

In a review, this part of the roadmap is connected back to the household's income needs, tax picture, risk comfort, liquidity, spouse protection, and future flexibility. The goal is to understand

how questions are welcome affects the broader plan before a decision is made.

The important issue is connection. A decision that seems small by itself can affect income, taxes, risk, spouse protection, healthcare flexibility, or future choices.

A better approach is to bring the question into the open. A review can sort what is clear, what needs confirmation, and what should be coordinated with another qualified professional.

The useful planning move is to connect the topic to real household cash flow. If the decision changes monthly income, liquidity, taxes, spouse protection, healthcare flexibility, or legacy intentions, it deserves a place on the roadmap.

A Client-Style Example

Before meeting with Kayla, a couple collects statements and benefit estimates and finds questions they did not know they needed to ask.

The couple's folder reveals more than numbers. It reveals old beneficiaries, a pension question, a life policy they had forgotten, and a Social Security estimate that needs updating.

The lesson is not that every reader with a similar story needs the same answer. The lesson is that personal context changes the planning conversation.

If a scenario feels familiar, it is worth writing down what part caught your attention and bringing that note to a review.

Common Misunderstandings

People often think they need perfect records before scheduling a review.

The advisor can work with imperfect information, but missing documents should be named.

A third misunderstanding is assuming the chapter topic can be decided by a rule of thumb. A rule of thumb may start a

conversation, but it cannot replace a review of income need, time horizon, health, family priorities, tax status, and comfort with tradeoffs.

What People Often Overlook

Old policies may still have value or obligations.

A simple spending estimate can be more useful than a perfect budget.

People also overlook how this issue interacts with the rest of the plan. Old policies may still have value or obligations.

People also overlook how this issue interacts with the rest of the plan. A simple spending estimate can be more useful than a perfect budget.

They also overlook how helpful simple organization can be. A folder of current statements, policy pages, beneficiary records, and benefit estimates can make a review far more productive.

What a Planning Review Usually Looks At

A preparation review identifies what is ready and what still needs to be gathered:

current and future income sources, including Social Security, pension income, employment income, annuity income, and portfolio withdrawals

essential expenses, lifestyle expenses, healthcare costs, debt payments, family support, charitable goals, and emergency reserves

account types, tax treatment, beneficiary designations, liquidity needs, market exposure, and protection strategies

insurance coverage, life insurance, long-term care concerns, Medicare planning, survivor income needs, and legacy intentions

The review should connect decisions rather than treating each topic as a separate island.

When your documents and questions are ready, or even partly ready, you can schedule the review at https://host.safemsngr.com/widget/bookings/psglifeandretirementplan.

Questions to Bring Into the Conversation

Use these questions to prepare for a more useful first meeting:

What documents are missing from our planning folder?

What worries do we want to discuss even if they do not show up on a statement?

Who else should be involved, such as a tax professional, attorney, or spouse?

They are not do-it-yourself instructions; they are prompts to bring into a qualified review.

A Calm Planning Note

Preparation turns a meeting from vague to useful. Even imperfect documents can help the advisor ask better questions.

A calm planning conversation should make the next step feel clearer. It may lead to action, or it may simply identify what should be watched, verified, or discussed with a tax, legal, Medicare, Social Security, or insurance professional.

What Good Preparation Really Does

Good preparation saves time, but more importantly, it improves the quality of the conversation. A current statement can show whether an account is traditional, Roth, taxable, inherited, or annuity-based. A policy page can reveal premiums, riders, surrender charges, death benefits, or long-term care features. A Social Security estimate can anchor a claiming discussion.

The reader should not avoid a review because one document is missing. Instead, the missing document should become part of the agenda. An advisor can often say, 'This is what we can discuss today, and this is what we need before making a decision.' That approach is far better than guessing.

Preparation should include questions as well as paperwork. A concern about a spouse, taxes, Medicare, market loss, long-term care, or children may be the most important item the reader brings.

It can also help to bring the most recent version of documents, not the most perfect version. A current statement, even if the reader does not fully understand it, gives the review a starting point. A policy page with confusing language can be translated. A tax return can raise questions for a qualified tax professional. A handwritten spending estimate can be refined. The point is progress, not perfection.

Chapter Summary

This chapter's key point is that what to gather before a retirement income review should be reviewed in context, not as an isolated decision.

The reader does not need to leave with a product decision. The better goal is to leave with clearer questions and a stronger understanding of what personal review should cover.

Next, the book explains how Price Services Group can help guide the conversation.

Chapter 16: How Price Services Group Can Help

A guide can help organize the conversation so retirement decisions feel less scattered.

Price Services Group, L.L.C. helps clients think through income, protection, safe money concepts, Medicare planning, Social Security timing, life insurance, long-term care concerns, and legacy goals in an educational, suitability-based way.

A Guided Conversation

The role of a guide is to help connect the pieces, explain tradeoffs, and identify where additional professional input may be needed.

Price Services Group can be positioned as a guide without turning the book into a sales brochure. The role is to help organize the income picture, explain safe money concepts, discuss insurance and annuity education, and identify where other professionals should be involved.

In a review, this part of the roadmap is connected back to the household's income needs, tax picture, risk comfort, liquidity, spouse protection, and future flexibility. The goal is to understand how a guided conversation affects the broader plan before a decision is made.

The important issue is connection. A decision that seems small by itself can affect income, taxes, risk, spouse protection, healthcare flexibility, or future choices.

A better approach is to bring the question into the open. A review can sort what is clear, what needs confirmation, and what should be coordinated with another qualified professional.

The useful planning move is to connect the topic to real household cash flow. If the decision changes monthly income, liquidity, taxes, spouse protection, healthcare flexibility, or legacy intentions, it deserves a place on the roadmap.

Education Before Decisions

A good process helps the client understand options before choosing among them. It does not require every person to use the same strategy.

A client-centered process usually starts with listening. Before strategies are compared, the conversation should clarify income needs, current resources, health concerns, family priorities, tax questions, Medicare issues, and comfort with risk.

In a review, this part of the roadmap is connected back to the household's income needs, tax picture, risk comfort, liquidity, spouse protection, and future flexibility. The goal is to understand how education before decisions affects the broader plan before a decision is made.

The important issue is connection. A decision that seems small by itself can affect income, taxes, risk, spouse protection, healthcare flexibility, or future choices.

A better approach is to bring the question into the open. A review can sort what is clear, what needs confirmation, and what should be coordinated with another qualified professional.

The useful planning move is to connect the topic to real household cash flow. If the decision changes monthly income, liquidity, taxes, spouse protection, healthcare flexibility, or legacy intentions, it deserves a place on the roadmap.

Where You Matter

The phrase Where You Matter is more than a line on a page. It reflects the idea that planning should begin with the person, not the product.

The phrase 'Where You Matter' should show up in the experience, not just on the page. That means plain language, patience, and recommendations that are suitable for the person in front of the advisor.

In a review, this part of the roadmap is connected back to the household's income needs, tax picture, risk comfort, liquidity, spouse protection, and future flexibility. The goal is to understand how where you matter affects the broader plan before a decision is made.

The important issue is connection. A decision that seems small by itself can affect income, taxes, risk, spouse protection, healthcare flexibility, or future choices.

A better approach is to bring the question into the open. A review can sort what is clear, what needs confirmation, and what should be coordinated with another qualified professional.

The useful planning move is to connect the topic to real household cash flow. If the decision changes monthly income, liquidity, taxes, spouse protection, healthcare flexibility, or legacy intentions, it deserves a place on the roadmap.

A Client-Style Example

A household arrives with uncertainty and leaves with a clearer list of issues to review, questions to ask, and next steps to consider.

A good first meeting does not have to end with a product. It can end with a clearer picture, a short list of issues to review, and a sense that the household has a guide.

The lesson is not that every reader with a similar story needs the same answer. The lesson is that personal context changes the planning conversation.

If a scenario feels familiar, it is worth writing down what part caught your attention and bringing that note to a review.

Common Misunderstandings

Asking for help does not mean surrendering control.

Education and suitability should come before product discussion.

A third misunderstanding is assuming the chapter topic can be decided by a rule of thumb. A rule of thumb may start a

conversation, but it cannot replace a review of income need, time horizon, health, family priorities, tax status, and comfort with tradeoffs.

What People Often Overlook

Some questions belong with a tax professional, attorney, Medicare specialist, or Social Security representative.

A second meeting may be necessary before decisions are made.

People also overlook how this issue interacts with the rest of the plan. Some questions belong with a tax professional, attorney, Medicare specialist, or Social Security representative.

People also overlook how this issue interacts with the rest of the plan. A second meeting may be necessary before decisions are made.

They may overlook the value of a second conversation. Many thoughtful decisions require time to review options, ask follow-up questions, and coordinate with tax or legal professionals.

What a Planning Review Usually Looks At

A Price Services Group conversation may review several connected planning areas:

current and future income sources, including Social Security, pension income, employment income, annuity income, and portfolio withdrawals

essential expenses, lifestyle expenses, healthcare costs, debt payments, family support, charitable goals, and emergency reserves

account types, tax treatment, beneficiary designations, liquidity needs, market exposure, and protection strategies

insurance coverage, life insurance, long-term care concerns, Medicare planning, survivor income needs, and legacy intentions

The review should connect decisions rather than treating each topic as a separate island.

To begin a personalized planning conversation with Price Services Group, use https://host.safemsngr.com/widget/bookings/psglifeandretirementplan.

Questions to Bring Into the Conversation

Use these questions to decide what kind of guidance would help:

What would a clear next step look like after the first conversation?

Which issues need education, and which need a specific professional recommendation?

How will we know whether a strategy truly fits our situation?

They are not do-it-yourself instructions; they are prompts to bring into a qualified review.

A Calm Planning Note

Guidance should feel steady and understandable. The client should know what is being discussed, why it matters, and what remains to confirm.

A calm planning conversation should make the next step feel clearer. It may lead to action, or it may simply identify what should be watched, verified, or discussed with a tax, legal, Medicare, Social Security, or insurance professional.

What Guidance Should Feel Like

A client-facing process should feel organized, respectful, and understandable. The reader should not feel rushed into a product or embarrassed for asking basic questions. Retirement income planning involves personal money, family obligations, health concerns, and hopes for the future. It deserves patience.

Price Services Group can help by organizing the income picture, explaining safe money strategies, educating clients about annuities and insurance concepts, discussing Social Security timing and Medicare planning considerations, and identifying where tax, legal, or other professional guidance may be needed. The exact services and recommendations should always depend on the client's situation and applicable licensing and compliance requirements.

The soft invitation is simple: if the reader wants help seeing how the pieces fit together, a personalized planning conversation can be scheduled. The book educates; the review personalizes.

That distinction is important. A book can explain concepts, but it cannot know the reader's exact income sources, health history, spouse needs, tax picture, insurance contracts, or comfort with risk. A planning conversation can take the education from these pages and apply it carefully to the household in front of the advisor.

The review may also identify questions that should be answered somewhere else. Tax questions may belong with a qualified tax professional. Estate documents may need an attorney. Medicare plan details may require current plan materials and Medicare-specific guidance. Social Security claiming questions may need current SSA information. A strong guide does not pretend to be every professional at once; a strong guide helps the client know which questions belong where.

That kind of coordination can be especially valuable for clients who have been collecting advice in fragments. One article says to delay Social Security. Another says to protect principal. A friend recommends a product. A family member worries about long-term care. The review gives those fragments a place to be sorted calmly. Some ideas may fit. Some may not. Some may need more information. The client should leave with a clearer path, not a heavier pile of opinions.

Chapter Summary

This chapter's key point is that how price services group can help should be reviewed in context, not as an isolated decision.

The reader does not need to leave with a product decision. The better goal is to leave with clearer questions and a stronger understanding of what personal review should cover.

Next, readers meet the author behind the guide.

Chapter 17: About the Author

Trust is built through clarity, care, and a process that treats people like people.

Kayla Price works through Price Services Group, L.L.C., guided by the brand phrase Where You Matter.

A Client-Centered Standard

Kayla Price and Price Services Group, L.L.C. approach planning conversations with an emphasis on clarity, education, and respect for the client's individual situation.

An author page should reassure the reader that the book came from a real client-service perspective. It does not need to overstate credentials or promise outcomes. It should reflect Kayla Price's commitment to education and personal attention.

In a review, this part of the roadmap is connected back to the household's income needs, tax picture, risk comfort, liquidity, spouse protection, and future flexibility. The goal is to understand how a client-centered standard affects the broader plan before a decision is made.

The important issue is connection. A decision that seems small by itself can affect income, taxes, risk, spouse protection, healthcare flexibility, or future choices.

A better approach is to bring the question into the open. A review can sort what is clear, what needs confirmation, and what should be coordinated with another qualified professional.

The useful planning move is to connect the topic to real household cash flow. If the decision changes monthly income, liquidity, taxes, spouse protection, healthcare flexibility, or legacy intentions, it deserves a place on the roadmap.

Why This Book Exists

This book exists because retirement income conversations often become complicated too quickly. Many families need a plain-language path into the discussion.

For many readers, the first appointment is less about buying something and more about finally saying the quiet questions out loud. That is a worthy starting point.

In a review, this part of the roadmap is connected back to the household's income needs, tax picture, risk comfort, liquidity, spouse protection, and future flexibility. The goal is to understand how why this book exists affects the broader plan before a decision is made.

The important issue is connection. A decision that seems small by itself can affect income, taxes, risk, spouse protection, healthcare flexibility, or future choices.

A better approach is to bring the question into the open. A review can sort what is clear, what needs confirmation, and what should be coordinated with another qualified professional.

The useful planning move is to connect the topic to real household cash flow. If the decision changes monthly income, liquidity, taxes, spouse protection, healthcare flexibility, or legacy intentions, it deserves a place on the roadmap.

The Invitation

Readers are invited to use this guide as a starting point for better questions and more organized planning conversations.

The author positioning should remain warm and modest: Kayla and Price Services Group are guides for a conversation that deserves care.

In a review, this part of the roadmap is connected back to the household's income needs, tax picture, risk comfort, liquidity, spouse protection, and future flexibility. The goal is to understand

how the invitation affects the broader plan before a decision is made.

The important issue is connection. A decision that seems small by itself can affect income, taxes, risk, spouse protection, healthcare flexibility, or future choices.

A better approach is to bring the question into the open. A review can sort what is clear, what needs confirmation, and what should be coordinated with another qualified professional.

The useful planning move is to connect the topic to real household cash flow. If the decision changes monthly income, liquidity, taxes, spouse protection, healthcare flexibility, or legacy intentions, it deserves a place on the roadmap.

A Client-Style Example

Readers who value a calm, educational conversation can use this chapter to understand the spirit behind the firm.

Readers should feel that Kayla's role is to explain, organize, and guide. Trust grows when people can ask basic questions without embarrassment.

The lesson is not that every reader with a similar story needs the same answer. The lesson is that personal context changes the planning conversation.

If a scenario feels familiar, it is worth writing down what part caught your attention and bringing that note to a review.

Common Misunderstandings

An author bio should not be read as a guarantee of results.

The relationship still begins with a personal review, not a book chapter.

A third misunderstanding is assuming the chapter topic can be decided by a rule of thumb. A rule of thumb may start a conversation, but it cannot replace a review of income need, time horizon, health, family priorities, tax status, and comfort with tradeoffs.

What People Often Overlook

Readers may need to verify current licensing, services, and state availability.

A warm relationship still requires clear disclosures.

People also overlook how this issue interacts with the rest of the plan. Readers may need to verify current licensing, services, and state availability.

People also overlook how this issue interacts with the rest of the plan. A warm relationship still requires clear disclosures.

What a Planning Review Usually Looks At

A review for this topic usually focuses on the facts that affect the household's next decision:

current and future income sources, including Social Security, pension income, employment income, annuity income, and portfolio withdrawals

essential expenses, lifestyle expenses, healthcare costs, debt payments, family support, charitable goals, and emergency reserves

account types, tax treatment, beneficiary designations, liquidity needs, market exposure, and protection strategies

insurance coverage, life insurance, long-term care concerns, Medicare planning, survivor income needs, and legacy intentions

The review should connect decisions rather than treating each topic as a separate island.

If Kayla's client-centered approach sounds like the guidance you want, use https://host.safemsngr.com/widget/bookings/psglifeandretirementplan to request a conversation.

Questions to Bring Into the Conversation

Use these questions as conversation starters for your own situation:

What kind of planning relationship helps us feel respected and heard?

Do we want a conversation that explains tradeoffs before presenting options?

What would make us feel more confident asking questions?

They are not do-it-yourself instructions; they are prompts to bring into a qualified review.

A Calm Planning Note

The author relationship begins with education, but trust grows through careful listening and clear next steps.

A calm planning conversation should make the next step feel clearer. It may lead to action, or it may simply identify what should be watched, verified, or discussed with a tax, legal, Medicare, Social Security, or insurance professional.

A Note on Trust

Trust in retirement planning is built through the small moments: explaining a term without making the client feel small, slowing down when a decision feels emotional, and being clear about what is educational versus what requires a personal recommendation. Readers should feel that asking questions is part of the process, not an interruption.

Kayla Price and Price Services Group are positioned in this book as guides. That matters because many families do not need more noise. They need someone to help organize the conversation, explain tradeoffs, and point out where additional professional review may be appropriate.

That guide role is especially important when the reader has been carrying questions quietly for years.

Chapter Summary

This chapter's key point is that about the author should be reviewed in context, not as an isolated decision.

The reader does not need to leave with a product decision. The better goal is to leave with clearer questions and a stronger understanding of what personal review should cover.

The final note explains why an annual update matters.

Bring This Book to Your Review

Bring this book with you to your retirement income review appointment. If you marked pages, wrote questions, or circled sections that felt important, we can use those notes to make the conversation more personal and productive.

Chapter 18: Annual Update Note

This 2026 edition is intended to be reviewed annually. Retirement income planning changes because Social Security figures, Medicare costs, tax rules, RMD rules, interest rates, annuity rates, product availability, market conditions, and household needs can change.

An annual review helps keep the income roadmap current instead of letting old assumptions guide new decisions.

Annual Review Checklist

Each year, consider reviewing:

☐ Social Security annual figures and benefit estimates

☐ Medicare premiums, deductibles, and IRMAA thresholds

Tax and RMD rule references

☐ Interest-rate environment and annuity rate assumptions

☐ Insurance and annuity product availability

☐ Retirement income needs and monthly cash-flow changes

☐ Market risk, inflation, and emergency reserve assumptions

Spouse/survivor income needs

☐ Long-term care concerns and family changes

☐ Booking link, contact information, and disclaimer language

Final Thought

Retirement income planning is not a one-time calculation. It is a living conversation about income, risk, taxes, healthcare, spouse protection, and future flexibility.

Price Services Group, L.L.C. | Where You Matter | priceservicesgroup.com

Retirement Income / Life & Retirement Planning Appointments: https://host.safemsngr.com/widget/bookings/psglifeandretirementplan

www.ingramcontent.com/pod-product-compliance
Lightning Source LLC
LaVergne TN
LVHW050826061126
851857LV00012B/993